There is Nothing Louder Than Silence
A Widow's Journey Through Grief

by Joanne D. Saunders

REVIEWS

When Joanne Saunders lost her husband suddenly, she found herself in a world forever altered. *There is Nothing Louder than Silence* is her honest account of facing grief head-on, embracing both its weight and its lessons. This book does not promise closure—it promises connection, understanding, and the small steps toward restoration that keep us moving forward.
Christine Droney, MSW, LCSW, N-CTTP, CT, PMH-C
Owner/Licensed Clinical Social Worker

There is Nothing Louder than Silence is a great read that is a Heartfelt personal journal of a love story, family and the curve ball that changes everything. Pure honesty, of the day-to-day challenges and strength derived from a death. R. Cobb

There Is Nothing Louder Than Silence invites readers on a heartfelt journey through Joanne Saunders' struggles as she navigates the ups and downs of losing her beloved husband. She shares her raw emotions while weaving in her personal background and faith throughout the book. This is an excellent read for those who have lost a loved one or for anyone seeking to support and better understand those who have.

Kelly O'Neill Kawczynski

Joanne Saunders delves into very personal aspects of her life and her journey with loss and grief. She validates the feelings of desperation, loss, loneliness, and sadness that are beyond comprehension for anyone who has never lost a spouse. I must admit I cried through most of the book, but I could not put it down. In navigating the emotional hurdles after the loss of her husband, she offers insight into how to get beyond the unimaginable grief. You never get over the loss of a loved one. You learn to live with it. This is where Joanne gives the reader hope.

"The journey of grief is not about forgetting or moving on; it is about embracing the silence, acknowledging the pain, and allowing ourselves to heal through the power of laughter, love, and tears."

My husband was a handsome, successful, loving man and a wonderful father to our sons. With little warning, he was diagnosed with terminal cancer. In less than six weeks, he was gone. He was the love of my life. I am the woman who was caring for the stray, pregnant kitten. I am proud and honored to call Joanne Saunders my friend.

Grace W. Rosenow

THERE IS NOTHING LOUDER THAN SILENCE
A Woman's Journey Through Grief

by Joanne D. Saunders

FOREWORD

When Joanne first told me she was writing this book, I knew it would be something special. I've had the privilege of knowing Joanne for many years, and her resilience, wisdom, and warmth have always been evident. Her journey through grief, healing, and rediscovery is nothing short of inspirational.

Grieving is a deeply personal and often isolating experience. Joanne's story is a testament to the power of vulnerability, courage, and the unwavering spirit to move forward. In these pages, you will find raw honesty, profound insights, and practical advice that can help anyone navigating the rough waters of loss.

Joanne's ability to blend heartfelt storytelling with practical tools and resources makes this book a valuable companion for anyone dealing with grief. Her unique perspective, grounded in both personal experience and empathy, offers comfort and guidance that is both relatable and actionable.

This book is not just about surviving loss; it's about thriving in the face of it. It's about finding light in the darkest of times and rediscovering the strength within. Joanne's journey is a powerful reminder that it's okay to feel, to stumble, and to start over as many times as needed. Her message is clear: you are not alone, and you are stronger than you think.

I am honored to introduce you to this incredible work and to Joanne's remarkable journey. As you read, may you find solace, hope, and the courage to move forward on your own path.

With heartfelt admiration,

Chris

ACKNOWLEDGEMENTS

Writing this book has been a journey of immense personal growth and healing, and I could not have done it alone.

First and foremost, I would like to thank Pat Saunders, whose love and memory have been a guiding light throughout this process. Though you are no longer physically with us, your spirit continues to inspire me every day.

To Beth Anne Barron, your unwavering strength and joy are a constant reminder of the importance of love and resilience. Caring for you has been both a challenge and a blessing, and I am grateful for your presence in my life.

I am deeply indebted to Christine Droney, my therapist, for her wisdom, guidance, and patience. Your support has been instrumental in helping me navigate the complexities of grief and rediscover my path forward. I could not have done this without you.

To my incredible network of friends and family: thank you for your endless support, understanding, and encouragement. My sons Stephen and Brian Saunders, my brothers and their wives, Ted and Jane Darocha, Barry and Kristin Crisci-Darocha, my dear friend and partner in crime, Kelly O'Neill Kawczynski, Grace and John Rosenow, Lillian Gaffney and all of the others who supported me behind the scenes, your kind words and actions have provided me with the strength to keep moving forward.

Finally, to everyone who has shared a kind word, a helpful resource, or a moment of understanding: you have my heartfelt thanks. This book is a testament to the power of community and the strength that comes from knowing we are not alone.

INTRODUCTION

Full disclosure here, if you bought this book looking for the answers, ask for a refund. I don't have the answers, but I will speak the truth, and maybe you won't feel so alone in this forced-upon life. I will try to dispel the myth of healing with time. Let's get this out of the way now, you never heal. If you have been told by caring friends and family that it will get better with time, my dear reader they are lying to you. I know this may sound harsh, but if you have expectations of being who you were before losing your spouse, you are only fooling yourself. Better is relative. Pull on your big girl panties and get ready to start to change, you've got a lot of evolving ahead. You are going to wear many hats, do things you thought you were never capable of doing, cry your heart out on the floor of your shower, have zero desire to do anything or conversely feel like you have to do it all.. You will literally be reinventing the wheel. Grieving is not a linear journey, no, it's more like scribbles on a page, it's all over the place. I shared this with my grief counselor, it may give you some clarity:

When a person loses a spouse, it takes time to redevelop, rebuild, and regain a fragment of who they were without that person in their life. It is a brand new journey for the widow, one she never expected to be on. While she may have a network of friends and family, a widow has never felt more alone.

After spending decades with your person, building your dreams, conquering the hurdles life throws your way together, sharing personal as well as physical intimacies, it takes more than just a short period of time to heal; and let's be honest, you never really heal, you change. So while outwardly the widow may appear to have it all together, inwardly she is still trying to put the pieces together. The widow is establishing new boundaries, discovering new means of survival, risking trust, feeling vulnerable.

Time to recover from the loss is irrelevant, but being able to adapt is everything.

The best advice I can give you, is you do you. You've just experienced a loss of limb and now you have to figure out how to live without it. As with any amputation, you carry with you a daily reminder of what you lost, and no prosthesis can replace it. So I invite you to sit back, grab a box of tissues, maybe a glass of wine or a warm cup of tea. Put your feet up and let me take you through my grief journey, maybe together we can find our way to the other side.

IN MEMORIAM

To my beloved husband, Pat, whose memory continues to inspire and guide me every day. Your love and support made me the person I am today, and your absence has taught me the depth of my own strength. I will always cherish our time together.

DEDICATION

To Beth Anne, my sunshine, whose boundless spirit and unwavering love remind me daily of the importance of compassion and resilience. You are my joy and my purpose.

To my incredible network of friends and family, who have provided me with endless support, love, and understanding. You have been my light in the darkest of times, and for that, I am eternally grateful.

CHAPTER 1

* * *

"On this day I married my friend, the one who shares my life, my love and my dreams."

Our Wedding Invitation

My husband was a noisy man. He was very vocal, grunting about this ache or that pain, talking to the pets, or just randomly talking out loud. When he coughed, he would make it sound like he was choking to death, just for the attention. Even in his sleep, he snored like a freight train barreling through the room. He would admit to people he just met, "I can't whisper," and he couldn't—his voice was naturally loud. I always knew he was in the house until that morning, January 11, 2022, when the noise stopped forever.

My day was starting early. The morning was like any normal morning. I was in the kitchen, doing my usual routine, and heard my husband stirring around in the bathroom upstairs. I could hear him moaning and groaning from the aches and pains that were well earned through sports, hard work, an active life, and some neglect. I didn't pay attention to it because it was a song he would sing daily. When I finished feeding the cats and emptying the dishwasher, I headed up to take my shower. The bathroom door was still closed, so I sat going through my emails and checking up on the latest posts on Facebook. I realized Pat was up early. His usual routine was to come down about an hour after I got up. He knew how much I enjoyed my quiet mornings. The fact that he was up early could only mean one thing: he was taking us out to breakfast. He was that type of guy; he would surprise you when you least suspected it. As I was feeding the cats, I heard an unusual, high-pitched "ooh" and thought to myself, "Oh, that wasn't a good move."

Pat was just a few replacements short of the Bionic Man (I am dating myself with that reference). He had a double knee replacement, a bad back, and a steel plate holding his femur together, which had been broken after a fall—a story for another book. He had epilepsy, arthritis, and clotting issues, which we suspected were genetic. All of this came from living a full life and not realizing the toll it was taking on his body. He would often tease that being so broken was the only way I could catch him, and what a catch he was!

I finished what I was doing in the kitchen, headed up to our room, and sat waiting for him to finish in the bathroom. I don't know how long it took me to realize that I didn't hear anything. There wasn't a sound coming from the room—no shower, no water running, no chorus of ooh's and ahh's. When I did realize, I rushed to the bathroom and saw my best friend, unresponsive, head down, eyes open, and drooling. In a brief second—a flash, really—I felt a little envious that he was in the loving arms of Jesus. I knew he was gone; there wasn't any question. But I knew every second counted, and I was going to fight for his life. I had to start the tug of war. How I managed to call 911 is beyond me. I was in fight or flight mode. I couldn't think clearly. I must have dialed it, or a combination of 911, at least three times. My fingers were shaking, my body trembling. I just couldn't seem to push the right sequence of numbers. I was living my worst nightmare.

The first thing I needed to do was lift a 237-pound man and lay him flat on the floor. You can do the impossible when the adrenaline is flowing. I had the 911 dispatcher on speaker. He could hear me saying to Pat, "This is going to hurt. I am sorry. I am doing my best." The dispatcher began coaching me to start CPR. It had been years since my last refresher course. As I was doing CPR, I could see color returning to his face. There was a glimmer of hope—or at least I thought. I began screaming for him to fight like he had never fought before. "Come on, Baby, I am here. Hear me? Fight, you son-of-a-bitch, fight!" I don't usually curse, but it flowed out of my mouth so freely. I checked for a pulse—nothing. As soon as I stopped the compression, the color faded from his face, his eyes a distant stare. I heard his ribs break under each push, and as I breathed air into his lungs, I could hear the rattling of fluid. I knew enough to know that was not normal and not a good sign. My mind told me he wasn't coming back, but I didn't stop trying to save him until the first responders made their way into the house. I don't know how long I performed CPR. My mouth was dry, my elbows trembling, but I was determined to keep going. When they took over, I went to the side of my bed, got down on my knees, and prayed, "God, I don't know where to begin, but help me through this." I got up off my knees, the room filled with police and EMTs. Everybody was asking questions: "What medications was he on?" "What is his health history?" "Does he have a living will?" "How old is he?" "Does he have a

DNR?" "How much do you want us to do?" I couldn't even think of answering them. The man I had shared my life, my love, and my dreams with, my best friend, just died, and I couldn't save him. I went downstairs to the hall bathroom and threw up. I sat on the bathroom floor, my body still trembling, my arms shaking from my attempt to revive my husband.

I came out of the bathroom to an officer standing in the kitchen, waiting for me. "Ma'am, I have the medical examiner on the phone. Nothing seems suspicious, but we have to determine the cause of death." Did I just hear that right? 'Nothing seems suspicious'? I just coded my husband, you fool, my mind was screaming at him. How dare you! I took his phone, heard a woman's voice. She gave me her name, but like a feather in the wind, it blew right away. She started by saying, "Mrs. Saunders, I am sorry for your loss." I've never hated a word more than I do 'sorry,' and a litany of sorries was on its way. Another barrage of questions came through the phone. Who is his primary care physician? Was he having any health issues? What medications was he on? Did he drink, smoke, take drugs? Can you describe how you found him? The fluid I heard in his lungs, I was told, was blood. She suspected he died from a massive clot that ruptured his heart. He was gone before he could finish saying 'Ooh.' Cause of death: natural. In an attempt to provide peace of mind, she said even if he had been in the hospital when this happened, there would have been nothing they could have done to save him. "You did your best."

Somewhere between praying, answering the same questions over again, and bringing up the empty void of my stomach, I had called my sons to let them know their dad had died. Two of the hardest phone calls I had to make. I can't remember the words they said, only the sound of denial, fear, and heartbreak echoed in their voices. My mouth was dry. I couldn't drink enough water to keep it moist. Time was racing by me, yet I was well aware that just a few hours ago, he was alive, and I was on a new journey of widowhood. No longer married, a piece of me was just ripped away. I was sucker punched in the heart. I am in this alone. The next question stopped me in my place. "Where do you want us to take the body?" My husband was no longer a person; he was a body. Just like that, his identity was gone. Everything he ever was, gone.

Let's catch our breath. That was a hard start, ripping off the bandaid, so to speak. I resigned from a 34-year teaching career to become the legal guardian of my adult cousin who has special needs. The timing of leaving my career could not have been better, as it was at the height of Covid. Our home was small, and Beth was using the compact den as her bedroom. I hung a curtain in the doorway for her privacy. Pat decided it was time to move; our taxes were high, our budget fixed, and we could hear gunfire and firecrackers going off from the George Floyd riots happening just blocks away in Philadelphia. We needed more room. In July of 2020, we made settlement on our dream home, moved in, and started our 'retirement years.' I was really too young to retire, and as I write this, I still have not reached retirement age, but it's getting closer. The pandemic allowed us to get settled, work on the house and yard, and become familiar with the community on drives to the grocery store or hardware store. I was just learning to quilt and I had a sewing area all to myself in our finished basement. By all accounts, we were happy. There wasn't a day that went by where I wasn't grateful for being here. I could often be heard saying, "I love this house and my town," like a recording set on replay. God had His hand in this move in every way and I was sure to thank Him daily.

In October of 2020, I was trying to motivate Pat to start walking. He was becoming very sedentary, watching TV, and sleeping in his recliner. I was nothing short of a pest, trying to get him to become more active. Our new community had some amazing walking trails. An old rail line was converted into a bike and walking trail, much of which was shaded, with gentle inclines, farm fields on both sides with towering cornstalks, and very beautiful country scenery. Even our neighborhood had its own trails with riparian habitats to attract a wide variety of bird species to keep insect levels low, and meandering streams to help with water flow during heavy rains. It was our idea of perfection.

After my nagging, he finally agreed he would start walking, but it was conditional—he needed new sneakers. We headed to the outlets and had to go up a flight of about eight steps to get to the Nike store. Pat was out of breath. As any good, caring wife would be, I was annoyed and gave him a piece of my mind. The lecture started, "If you didn't sit around all day, you wouldn't have this problem." I could not possibly have known that this was the first sign of a bigger issue. About a day or two later, Pat was helping me do the laundry. He had just cleaned the toilet and was walking about 12 feet into the laundry room. He couldn't catch his breath. I had him breathe into a paper bag, thinking he was hyperventilating. I put my Apple Watch on him and started to track his EKG and took his blood pressure. I was a biology teacher and knew enough to know that what I was seeing was not a normal EKG and BP. I waited an hour after his breathing regulated, took it again, and was still seeing an irregularity, but I didn't know what it meant. I printed off both EKGs and we headed to the Urgent Care facility. Yes, there was something wrong—he needed to go to the emergency room immediately. Hours later, the doctor told us his condition was critical. He had a saddle clot in the heart extending to the pulmonary arteries. He should have been dead. The treatment was to administer tPA, a high risk clot busting drug. The risk we were taking was a do or die. If he had any weakened arteries anywhere, he could have an aneurysm that would kill him on the spot. We decided on the risk and Pat was admitted to intensive care for observation.

Being an epileptic, Pat was on a specific medication that didn't play too well with other medications and foods. He had already experienced a toxic reaction from anesthesia for his double knee replacement, went toxic when prescribed an antibiotic, and couldn't drink grapefruit juice without it impacting his levels negatively. We had a 100-page manuscript with 800 food and drug interactions that he could not have while taking this antiseizure medication. It was a small price to be seizure-free and, as his doctor put it, a 'poster child/adult' for the neurology department. Because of this, there was only one type of blood thinner Pat was able to take for his clotting, and he had to inject himself in the stomach two times a day. A thirty-day supply was over $1,000, and that is with medical insurance. The price of being alive was worth it.

One morning as he was dressing, I saw his abdomen just covered in bruises on both sides from the injections. But what I didn't know was that by November of 2021, he was cutting the dose in half to save money. When I caught him, I made an appointment with our primary care physician to have him seen and to let the doctor read him the riot act. Pat's response to me was,

"Only the good die young. God doesn't want me yet," and he believed it.

The week before he died, we were busy with the final steps for guardianship for Beth. Our lawyer felt it best that we both become her guardians in case something happened to either one of us. After our meeting, we went out to lunch and started to make plans to do day trips to explore more of the area where we had moved. I was excited. He was making healthier choices and buying into increasing his activity. Covid was somewhat behind us and it was time to do the things we had been talking about doing—together.

* * *

"Mrs. Saunders?" the police officer asked, "where do you want the body to be taken?" The EMTs had left, and Pat was still lying on the bathroom floor, with our sons, Stephen and Brian by his side.

"I don't know. We are new here, I don't know where he should go." He listed names of funeral homes that meant nothing to me until he came to one named Spacht. In Polish (my father's side of the family is from Poland and that was one of the few words I knew), Spacht means sleep. I picked that one. I went up to the bathroom and sat on the floor with him and the boys. Signs of how hard the EMTs worked to revive him were evident. I rubbed his chest and saw the gray color change in his face, the pooling of blood in his arms from lying on the floor for so long. I relived the noises, cracking of the ribs, gurgling in the lungs, putting my lips over his to force air into him, and I whispered, "I did everything I could to keep you here with us, but God was stronger." God was stronger.

As part of my Catholic upbringing, I knew it was important to have the last rites administered. It was a cleansing of the soul to be able to enter heaven. When I was with my aunt when she passed, I missed this part and was asked hours later by a priest if someone had come to give her the last rites. So, of course, I was going to have this done for my husband. What happened next was beyond anything I could have imagined. I could not have anticipated the proverbial slap in the face that was about to happen. I called our parish priest, told him Pat had died, and asked if he could come over for a blessing and pray with us. He said no. Yes, you read that right—no. It was 8:30 in the morning, and he couldn't because he had a funeral at 2 PM. "I am sorry, Joanne, for your loss. We don't come out for last rites anymore." "Fr., I don't know what to do." This was a tipping point in my shock. "They will call me when he arrives at the funeral home."

I spent 30 years teaching in the Catholic School System. I had close friendships with several priests. I was a director for a teen retreat known as Kairos, which I was involved in for 8 years. I have done service trips, volunteered for the church. Pat was a CYO coach for several years, and played Santa for the Catholic elementary school and community. Never once in those years did a priest tell us no. He could not be there for us. When my father died in 2018, our priest came to the house, blessed my father, prayed with my brothers and me, and counseled us on what to do next. He was there physically and spiritually for us.

This priest said, no. He didn't send a deacon, he didn't send a fellow parishioner. We had no support. I had a bottle of Holy Water from the National Shrine of the Basilica of Mary in Washington, DC. Pat, Beth, and I had recently done a day pilgrimage there. I got it, sprinkled it over him, and prayed the most nonsensical prayer I have ever prayed. I was befuddled, lost and very broken. Sometime later, I spoke with a priest from that parish (who had been transferred a few months prior), and he was just as perplexed as I was as to why his former colleague did not come to the home. He reassured me that my blessing was just what my husband needed, and much more meaningful. This was an assault on the foundation of not only my faith but also our sons' faith. They stopped going to church; it was their last straw.

Family and friends began to filter their way into our home, bringing tons of food and asking what they could do to help, and I was just numb. I still couldn't quench my thirst. I can't tell you how many bottles of water I had that day, but the state of shock gave me such a dry mouth. I had no appetite but felt it would be rude if I didn't eat something. Nothing had any taste to it. They were talking to me, but I could barely focus on what they were saying. I hadn't had a moment to process what just happened. I was swept up in the rapid current of loss. The room was noisy, and I was screaming in my mind for silence. I was mentally telling them all to shut up (using the words shut up for me is like dropping the f-bomb, I rarely used it, but I was thinking it loudly now). Don't you know the magnitude of what I just went through? I felt so alone, despite having a full house. My brothers and my son's girlfriend were amazing. They picked up on my state of mind and carried the conversations for me. They cleaned up when everyone left, spent time with my sons helping them to process what had just happened. Brian was having a hard time; he and his father were just on the path of mending some problems they had. Stephen was feeling guilty he didn't take his dad's call the day before. We were all processing the loss of the same man, but he played different roles in our lives. Where had the day gone? I could only tell you I was just hours away from having my husband with me, but it already felt like a lifetime that he was gone.

CHAPTER 2

That Day *Right in the middle of our life, on an ordinary day, the unthinkable happened. Everything went from ordinary to chaotic and there I stood, in the mess of it all, knowing there will now forever be a before and an after. Sharyn Marsh*

Twenty-seven years of marriage, some didn't think it would last five, gone. He honored his vows, till death do us part. What do you think heaven is like? Do you even think there is a heaven? I was wondering if he could see me, if he could see us, and how broken we all were.

I wanted to be mad at him. I wanted to have him back, but there was a part of me that knew he was without pain, feeling healthy and vibrant. I wouldn't have him back to be with me if he had to come back to that—and that pissed me off even more. I pictured him surrounded by his mom and dad, and those loved ones that left us all too early. I thought of him being with his first wife, and my loss felt so much greater. Who does he belong to, her or me?

Pat was a widower. His wife of a year and a half had been killed by a teenage drunk driver. After her death, he took a downward spiral: became an alcoholic, had anger issues, neglected himself, his family, and his friends. He would be out drinking at all hours, his seizures were uncontrolled, and he was taking 20 phenobarbital pills a day—he should have been passed out from the booze and medication. He was a mess. I had known Pat since I was nine (I will share that story with you a bit later). He was devastated at the loss of his wife. And to add icing to the cake, shortly after her death, his father suddenly passed away from the same thing that took Pat.

I had always admired the love that Pat had for his first wife. And through our marriage, I made sure that we remembered her with that love. I encouraged him to visit the gravesite several times during the year. I planted yellow flowers in her memory in the garden. During the holidays, I purchased an ornament we hung on the tree in memory of her. She was very much a part of the man I loved, and I wasn't there to take her place, but to love everything about him.

Barbara was quite a bit older than my husband—eleven years, to be exact. She went through a very difficult divorce from an abusive, alcoholic husband with whom they had three children together. Pat met her through his business and fell in love with her and her kids. He did everything with them: coached their sports teams, took them to baseball games, treated them as if they were his own. When they decided to marry, the Monsignor at the parish they attended would not agree to an annulment for Barbara, despite the abuse she and her kids endured. If Barbara was willing to make a significant monetary donation, then of course she would have the annulment. This put a bad taste in Pat's mouth towards the Catholic church, so they got married by a justice of the peace at their side yard on the rainiest day of the year. With patience and persistence, I am persistent, I helped Pat renew his faith and return to the church.

So, here I am, a cradle Catholic, widowed and wondering what did all of this mean after he passed away? Barbara was his first wife; he never stopped loving her. Was he back with her in heaven? Have I lost him totally? What does my faith tell me? What do I believe? Why did this happen now when God surely moved us here to start over? Why would He give us all of this and then take it away? God, I can't trust You anymore. Nothing makes sense, I have lost my peace of mind and soul.

* * *

I don't know how I managed to sleep through the night; the room was so silent it was deafening. I know I reached for him and his side of the bed was empty. I turned on the small fan just to have some white noise—I use that fan every night now to break up the silence. My brothers were up, coffee brewing, breakfast ready, talking with my oldest son, Stephen. We had an appointment with the funeral home, and I had a call I needed to make before we went. I called the priest at our old parish and told him what had happened. He was dumbfounded as well, but had the answer I needed to hear: "We'll have the funeral here."

One of the benefits of being a Catholic educator was that I taught the daughters of our hometown's funeral director. I knew him very well. Father recommended I give him a call, and he would work with us to set up the funeral. Pat wanted to be cremated, so that made it easier to get him to our former parish, which was 80 miles away. At 11:00 AM, we made our way to the funeral home. If it wasn't for the level-headedness of my brothers, I don't think I would have known what to do. I probably would have been ready for that padded room, just sitting there muttering to myself and blowing bubbles. I was clueless. I couldn't afford a funeral—we had just put our savings into a new home—and I was very much in the fog of grief and still in a state of shock.

I think what stood out for me the most and still does today is that my husband's life came down to deciding what type of cardboard box he would be cremated in. A cardboard box. Did I want him to have a pillow? Did I want it lined with fabric? What kind of cardboard did I want?
Are you f-ing kidding me? You can't make this stuff up. Deciding how your loved one will be cremated is the most violating part of the process. The dryness of my mouth came back; thank God they had soft mints on the table—I think I ate them all. Ninety-nine dollars for a corrugated cardboard box that you could probably buy at U-Haul for twenty bucks, was what it came down to. Throw in the pillows and lining, and you are talking $500, and it was going to be incinerated. No matter how compassionate and professional the funeral home staff was, you felt like you were being flouted.

Death certificates were twenty dollars a pop. How many do you think you'll need? How the hell am I supposed to know that? I've never been a widow before, what do I need them for? You'll need one to probate the will. When do I need to probate the will and how do I do that? We can sign you up with one of our 'after care' specialists and they could help you. Do I get a discount on that service if I buy the $500 corrugated box? Do you think they could hear these thoughts loudly racing through my mind? Were my facial expressions giving them a hint of the insanity I was feeling about all of this? Is this what his life came down to, a cardboard box?

Holy shit, how did I get here, but better yet, how do I get out?

We got through the initial planning. Our funeral home director would coordinate with Spacht. The boys could see their father in a visiting room before he was cremated. His marble box—because the cemetery will only bury marble—was Eagles green, his favorite NFL team. The boys chose that. We brought him back to the house and placed him on the mantel. He was home for a short time, but at least he was in the house with us and not in a refrigerated morgue. There would be no viewing, but there would be a receiving line for family and friends to offer their condolences before the funeral mass. The funeral will be Saturday, so family members can travel. We had it live streamed for those who could not make it.

    Let me talk a moment about the receiving line. Why is it part of the process? It is nothing but pure torture. Who came up with it and thought it was a good idea? How many times do I have to hear, "I am sorry for your loss"? I know they are sorry and want to support the family. I know they lost someone too when Pat died—that's why they are here. Then there are the people in line, who you don't know—that you should know—but the grief fog won't let you remember who the hell they are. Each new person lifts the floodgates of the dam, and the tears go flowing out. You catch your breath, and up comes someone else. I only remember what one person said to me out of the hundred or so people that attended. It was a long-time family friend of my husband and brother. He hugged me so tightly and said, "I should have told you this before now. Thank you for bringing my friend back to me. Thank you for helping him to find himself."

The end of the receiving line is in sight. I think I have a 13-gallon bag of used Kleenex I will have to take out with me, along with a half a dozen empty bottles of water. And go figure, in that moment, I can hear my mom saying, "The more you cry, the less you pee," and I am saying to myself, "You must be right, Mom." Like where did that come from?

While we are sitting in the pews waiting for the funeral director and his staff to get everything situated, I feel a hand on my shoulder, a warm sensation moves through my shoulder, chest, belly and down both arms. I turn to see who is behind me and my brother gives me a reassuring smile, but there's no one who had their hand on me. Is Pat with me? Was that him letting me know he was there? Am I losing it? The priest gave a touching account of Pat, his involvement with the church, playing Santa Claus for the school, coaching, ushering. It was really beautifully personal. Stephen did the eulogy, had us laughing and crying. We went to the gravesite. He was buried with his parents, and then to the wake. It was over, everything I dreaded was done. The drive home was silent. No Pat singing off key with the music, messing up the lyrics, talking sports with his sons, no coughing, moaning, no big warm hand to hold. The silence was getting louder.

Family left the next day. We had a ton of food in the fridge, but no one felt like eating it. I couldn't pull myself to go through the mass cards. I was tired of crying. I was craving alone time. It was the fourth day of widowhood and the after was about to begin. I was four days further away from the love of my life. The house smelled like a funeral home with all of the flowers and care baskets, a constant reminder of the empty void. I couldn't go into the bathroom without seeing him lying on the floor. The sounds and smells of that morning came rushing back like a raging bull. I scrubbed and cleaned, brought in different accents and plants, but every time I entered the room, he was there. I was screaming at him to fight. The cracking and gurgling pounded with my pulse in my ears. I turn on the shower, climb in, and sit on the floor sobbing. It's Sunday, I have to go to church, I need to pull myself together.

Stephen did not want me to attend mass alone. While he didn't really want to go, he wanted to look the priest in the eye and let him see the family he let down. It was surreal going to church without Pat. I felt like you could look at me and see my other half missing, despite the repair and restoration attempt I made with my make-up and hair. Part of me wished there was someone there I could tell them Pat had passed away, but we only knew a handful of people, and those we got close to already knew. Mass started, we're going through the motions and Father looks directly at us. He didn't appear to remember. The priest gave no indication that I had spoken to him just a few days prior to tell him my husband had died. Absolutely no recognition as we passed him on the way out after mass. And yet, the lector announced the passing of Patrick Saunders and asked to keep our family in their prayers. I was mortified. My church was failing me at the most crucial time of my life. Why am I here?

Even though we had tried to be active in our new parish, roadblocks abounded. Covid had us social distancing. The church bazaar was all online. Maybe we could donate something. I had quilted items that surely someone would buy. I was hit with another no, we do not take items like that for the bazaar. Okay, let's put a basket together, I prodded Pat to do. We looked at the basket ideas, saw there was a lack of items that might interest men, so we put together a fishing tackle basket, which we spent $120 to pull together. After the bazaar was over, the church bulletin had everybody's name in it who made donations, except for ours. We weren't looking for a thank you, but it was odd to be left off the list. In a year's time, we made friends with only one couple from the parish. They did their best to introduce us, since the woman in charge of the welcome committee never reached out to us, but the church community had their established cliques. I guess I should have expected the priest to exhibit the same indifference. I could no longer find my strength in the church. We did not feel welcome, we couldn't find our niche within the parish, and now after Pat's passing, I had no desire to continue to try.

Halfway through the week following Pat's passing, our young neighbor reached out to see how we were doing. I broke down with the disappointment and the lack of support I was getting from my parish, and they recommended a different Catholic church just a little further away. That Sunday, Brian, Stephen, Beth and I walked into the doors of the church I now call home. You could feel the community spirit. We were greeted and embraced by the church, and God in His strange sense of humor gave me a connection I never would have anticipated. I had taught the niece of the priest of the parish. They needed a Kairos director and look who just walked into the door. Two prayers were answered that day.

CHAPTER 3

"I don't wanna live without you, I don't wanna even breathe, I don't wanna dream about you. Wanna wake up with you next to me. I don't wanna go down any other road now, I don't wanna love nobody but you. Looking in your eyes now, if I had to die now, I don't wanna love nobody but you."--Blake Shelton

I think we need a break. Let me take this chapter to tell you our love story. I think you will enjoy it. It has the ingredients of a Hallmark movie. Pat was seven years older than me. He was my oldest brother's best friend. They played high school and college baseball together. They were both exceptional players and scouted to play for the Philadelphia Phillies. Neither accepted the offer. I was just nine years old when I told my friend Maria my biggest secret—I had a crush on Pat. Out of all of my brother's friends, he was one of the few who didn't treat me as "Ted's little sister." I was a person. So, of course, how could you not have a crush on that?

Maria and I had been playing truth or dare, and I took the dare. She dared me to ask Pat for a kiss. On one hot summer afternoon, after a baseball game, Pat came walking through the garage in his baseball uniform, cleats ticking on the cement, going to cool off in our pool with the team. I mustered up the courage and approached him with the dare. He bent down, gave me a kiss on the cheek, and promised me that when I turned sixteen, he would take me out for my first date. If there was music dubbed in, I think I would have heard Fred Astaire singing, "I'm in Heaven."

Unfortunately for me, he was unable to keep that promise. Not by any account of his own, my father's business relocated us to upstate New York, and while Ted kept me updated on the happenings of everything Pat, that dream didn't seem in reach. Around the time of my eighteenth birthday, Ted surprised me with the news that Pat was coming to New York to take me out on that date he promised. He was newly engaged to Barbara and told her he had to honor a promise he made to a young girl nine years prior. We had a fabulous night together, went to a campground where friends were camping. Sat around the bonfire, shared stories, laughed, and danced to Paul McCartney and Wings' "Silly Love Songs." He told me that whenever he hears that song, he would think of me.

College came and went. I had gotten engaged and broke it off. Moved back to Pennsylvania and started my teaching career. Ten years had passed. I had still kept an ear to the happenings of Pat. I heard he had lost his wife shortly after they married. His dad retired early to help him with his business, and after having hip replacement surgery, died from a clot moments after Pat left him, saying, "Dad, I am finally pulling my life back together." It was then that he dove deeper into alcohol, cigarettes, and the phenobarbital fog. A sweet Manhattan was a chaser to his drug. I can't say he was functioning at that time, but somehow he was surviving.

Re-entering the story was me, now 28 years old. I had purchased a used car and thought the dealership was taking advantage of me. I needed an honest mechanic, and Pat might have been in the trenches of grief and depression, but he was honest. I showed up at his repair station, very different from the 18-year-old he last saw. I had a southern accent from living in Tennessee for my college years and then some. He called me Nashville. I reminded him of the person he used to be before the cruelty of death found its way into his dreams and turned his world upside down.

Depression and loss had not been kind to him. He had gained weight, lost some hair, and had deep, dark circles under his eyes. But somewhere in those brown eyes, I could see a flicker of the old Pat still trying to burn its way out. In the hope of restoring some light to his life, I attempted to reunite Pat and Ted. As life would have it, marriage, jobs, and living out of state impeded their ability to remain connected. So what better way to have them get together than to go to a Phillies game? Pat had season tickets that he shared with his mom. The plans were set. At the last minute, Ted had to back out because of an issue at work, and I took his spot. Being transparent, I need to tell you Pat was dating a woman who had a young daughter with cerebral palsy. They were living at his house. I knew this and drew the line in the sand—this was just two old friends getting together and nothing more would come of it. I could not become the "other woman." I wouldn't want that done to me; I couldn't do it to anyone else. He agreed. We had a fabulous time—two very comfortable souls together.

I was teaching summer school at a Christian Brothers' reform school a couple of months after our baseball outing. It was an intense experience teaching teenage criminals, murderers, drug dealers, and thieves. It was a challenge, but a very fulfilling challenge. Nothing I had ever anticipated in doing, but I was busy and honing my teaching skills. So it was a surprise when I got a call out of the blue. It was Pat. Can we see each other for a drink?

I reminded him of my friendship rule, and he followed by, "I need to talk with you." He had broken it off with his girlfriend. He couldn't get me out of his mind. I made him feel like he hadn't felt in a very long time. The nine-year-old girl inside of me, fulfilling that dare, was saying, "Hot dang, yes!" But the woman inside of me was saying, "Fantasy crushes never come true—or do they?"

Sparing the details, we had a turbulent dating period. He had difficulty overcoming his depression, drinking, and staying out all night habits. His seizures were not being managed, and he was putting himself and others at risk by driving and working on automobiles despite the laws that were in place. If he went to the doctors, he would lose his license. After much research, his mother and I finally found a doctor who we felt could work with Pat. He went through all of the neurological testing. Pat could talk to you while he was having a seizure, and if you didn't recognize the telltale signs, you wouldn't know it. He would start shaking his leg, tilt his head to the right, clench his fist, and his eyes would glaze over a bit, like he was looking right through you. An untrained eye would miss this. The doctor was fabulous. He got him on the proper medicine regimen, and Pat became seizure-free for over thirty years! Praise God!

In between all of this, we broke up. It was his doing. He made sure he insulted me well because he knew that was the only way I would leave him. I was heartbroken, to say the least.

Three months later, I picked up the phone to make a call my brother asked me to make, I misdialed and the voice through the line said, "Joanne, this is Pat." I quickly fumbled for words, "I can't talk to you, I am just getting back on my feet." I got ready to hang up, and I heard him softly say, "Please."

Over those three months, I was praying continually. "God, if this is what you want for me, please give me peace in my heart—then I will know it is right." Every day I felt more unsettled than the last. I said yes and met him for drinks. Apologies abounded, groveling accepted, answers to why, acknowledgment of stupidity, every way he could beat himself up for hurting me was out in play. Bases were loaded; could I ever take him back for a second chance? I did, of course, but I told him I wasn't getting back into the game to be hurt again. It had to be all or nothing.

Here's where the story gets fun to tell. I can't tell you the number of times we have shared it. As I am typing away, I am smiling ear-to-ear. My parents were out of town and needed us to check on their house, water the plants, and get their mail. They lived two hours away, so we decided to spend the weekend there.

Pat wanted to sleep with me, and I let him but clearly said there would be no sex. He honored that request. No pressure—he just held me as I slept. The next day we went to the mall, and we were looking at some Swarovski Crystal. The next thing I know, he's buying a crystal Eagle, down on one knee, promising me that like this eagle, our love will soar. A crowd of people were gathering around and cheering us on.

  A few weeks later, he was going to ask my dad for my hand in marriage. My mother knew it was coming and secretly told me my dad was going to say no. What do you mean, no? I asked. My mom laughed at my question and reminded me of the competitiveness once shared between him and my brother. Well, before Ted and Pat played baseball together, they played on opposite teams. Ted was pitching for the first time and Pat stole home on him and the rest of Ted's pitching game was off. Dad never forgot the impact it had on my brother and he was going to make Pat pay, one way or the other. Okay, we can work with that, I thought. By now I was teaching at an all girls college preparatory school. I went to the athletic director and asked if I could borrow home plate and explained to her why I needed it, with her blessings we bagged it up and we were ready to ask away. When Pat asked my dad to marry me, and my dad said no, Pat handed him home plate. My dad shook his head with a sly smile and said, "no, you didn't steal home base from me, you stole it from her brother. He's the one you need to ask." All right, not as easy as I thought, but still workable. We went to Modell's and not only got home plate, we got first, second, third base and the pitchers mound so we would have "all of our bases covered". That is how a childhood crush and dream became a twenty seven year marriage to the man who shared my life, my love and my dreams, my friend. Our wedding song was Celine Dion's Power of Love. The old Pat was back, but new and improved.

CHAPTER 4

"Life isn't about how to survive the storm, but how you dance in the rain." Vivian Greene

Hard times can either push you apart or pull you together. It did both for us. At the height of the storm, we were two separate boats trying to stay afloat, but when the eye was overhead, we realized we couldn't do it by ourselves and that is putting it mildly. Let me cut to the chase and tell you *rock bottom has a basement*, you can always get lower than you expect. We lived in that basement for ten years. But the ten years prior to that, God allowed us to assist Him in two true miracles. After being told conception was nearly impossible for us, I became pregnant with our first miracle, Stephen; and two and a half years later when the doctor was going to say no again, we were blessed with our second miracle, Brian. Love took on a whole new dimension. And let me just add, cloning is possible, Brian is just like his dad and I said that the minute he was born, "I cloned my husband". Twenty-five years later, that has not changed.

During those first 10 years of our little family, we did all of the ritual family things together. The boys did T-ball, karate, track, lacrosse, and baseball. Our trunk was packed for outdoor events, Pat coached, I cheered. One of Pat's greatest pleasures was playing Santa for the community, church and friends. You can't have Santa without Mrs. Claus. A one time fill in, became 9 years of callbacks. Pat enjoyed it so much more than me, but I supported him regardless.

Sparing you the sorted details, things turned quickly for the worse. The loss of my mother, diagnosis of Alzheimers for my dad, unemployment, health issues for my husband, which included a 24 day hospital stay after breaking his femur, complications included hemorrhaging, clotting, an allergic reaction to medications and a toxic reaction with his seizure medication. While going through all of this, I received a letter, the step children were suing us for our house. Their mother died in 1981, they wanted the current market value of the home. We had just paid off the mortgage and now were forced to take out an equity loan to pay $60,000 in legal fees, estate assessments, we-I should say I-had to gather all of the receipts for all of the upkeep that was done to our 135 year old home, find the paperwork on the estate settlement from a lawyer who was now deceased, and retain a lawyer, all while Pat was recovering in the hospital. It turned out they would have owed us for maintaining the property for more than the value of the home, so they dropped the suit and promised to relinquish any future interest in the home. With only one income, we started to roll the dice to see which bill would get paid, we were facing foreclosure on the loan, started the paperwork for bankruptcy, our electricity was turned off multiple times, far too many to count, pb & j's became our staple meal, and our youngest son attempted suicide. Toward the end of our tenure in rock bottom's basement, my father passed away and Pat's mother was diagnosed with the same mind-stealing disease and then died as a result of nursing home neglect. Beth's care was also a critical concern. My parents had been her legal guardian, her options were limited to an institutionalized group home living, going to North Carolina to live with her brother and wait 7 years to be accepted into a support program, or to live with us. At the generosity of my husband, we chose the latter. We applied and were approved for a waiver to help support her needs.

A year after taking her into our home, I had celebrated my 30th year of teaching with the Sisters of Mercy. Under the new administration, that summer they asked me to resign my position and I assumed full-time care of my cousin and was approved as her in-home community support specialist. A role that dug us out of poverty and enabled us to initiate our move. God was guiding our every step. We put our house up for sale, which one step-son tried to prevent us from doing but was unsuccessful and we bought our dream home. July 2020 we were out of the basement and living on answered prayers.

I was given a year and a half to dance in the storm with my husband, in our new home, before God called Him home. In that time, we did a lot of repairing of a very stressed, injured relationship, that was so exhausted and weary. We were falling in love again. I think it is important to tell you, at one point during the tough times, I did consider divorce, there was a period where Pat had extreme anger issues. He punched Brian in the head and put his fist to my face. I drew the line in the sand and was ready to leave with the boys in tow. After a month or two of my consistent stance to not allow him to verbally and physically abuse us, Pat (and I got help). We discovered that the anger problem was nothing Pat had control over, it was an interaction with, you guessed it, that darn seizure medication. A medication adjustment, anger management and counseling and we were back on track.

* * *

Our refrigerator was full, but we needed the basics, and we had our fill of leftovers. Other than church I hadn't left the house. We made it a family outing. When you are in the state of grieving, you have the realization that the world doesn't stop going just because your world has. You observe people from a different point of view. This is going to sound counterintuitive, but as much as you have difficulty focusing, you are acutely aware of the little things. Those things that you would normally shake off are surprisingly irritating and loud. Your patience quota is running on empty, intolerance is a new companion and you suddenly acquired the feeling of vulnerability and it is stifling. I did not anticipate these feelings and when we got into the grocery store, I ran into a wall of emotions, with fear and anxiety at the top of the list. Children crying for their mothers to buy them something was like taking your fingernails down a chalkboard. I watched a man shake away the grasp of his wife's hand and I whispered under my breath, "if you only knew". The store wasn't crowded, but I felt closed in and I couldn't wait to get out. If I caught the glance of someone looking at me, I became insecure and wondered if they could tell I was a widow. Was it tattooed on my head, in my expression, the way I carried myself? I felt like it was a plague that there was no cure for and I was contagious. The physique of a man reminded me of Pat, even down to his gait. Could it be? No, no you fool, it's not. Someone walks by with a familiar cologne and it steals your breath. "I couldn't take it any longer, let's get out of here," I said to my oldest.

By the end of the week, Stephen returned back to work. Brian decided to continue college more locally so he could commute from home and the silence settled in. There was no TV show set to a program or movie that we hadn't seen 100 times over. No snoring from the chair, no cough or singing to himself in the kitchen when he was assembling a masterpiece sandwich. He could make shit look like it tasted amazing. His seasoning techniques were beyond comparison. I avoided sitting in his recliner, or touching anything that was his. I got up in the morning and stayed in my pajamas all day. I would catch myself just sitting and staring, doing nothing for hours. The get up and go person that I had been, was a sloth on the couch. I attended to those things that required immediate attention, but once that was done, the lump on the log resumed her position.

I forced myself to go into the bathroom. I would go in, but I wouldn't turn on the lights. I continued to have flashbacks every time I walked into the room. I called my brother, Ted, and asked if he would come help me paint my room and bathroom. I needed to try to change the look entirely. My neighbor came over and helped me pick out a color that I would not have normally chosen—Williamsburg Blue by Benjamin Moore, which has a green hue to it. I love it. I found my way into my sewing nook and made myself a new quilt for a bedspread. It was time for me to leave the house again. I had to run some much-needed errands. Both Beth and I needed refills on our prescriptions, I had to pick up the paint and supplies, and I needed coordinating fabric for the quilt. This time it would just be me (and Beth).

I consider myself a very self-sufficient person. During our basement years, I did a lot of the work on my own. Pat was suffering from depression, spent most of his day sleeping in his chair, and was skilled at giving directions, my commander and chief. If something was going to get done, it was all on my shoulders. If it went wrong, it was all my fault. I became very adept at problem-solving and making the impossible possible. You would think this would have prepared me for this day, but nothing can prepare you for losing a large part of yourself. Despite our hurdles, how we handled our stress, we were friends and lovers. He was every bit a part of me and I was only beginning to learn just how much that was. Every time I stepped out on my own, I felt a foreboding fear. What if I get lost? What if the car breaks down? What if I suddenly get sick? Who do I call if I need help? I felt like Bill Murray in *What About Bob*, the scene where he is trying to gain the courage to leave his home and then finding out his new psychiatrist is going to Lake Winnipesaukee for the summer. My anxiety level was immeasurable.

Beth and I headed out, and we decided to stop and pick up Brian's favorite kind of Italian coffee. As we were pulling out of the coffee shop, a fire truck went by with sirens blaring. I had a tightness in my chest. My breathing was rapid, and a feeling of fear crushed me. I couldn't move. I couldn't drive. I just sat there and broke down into tears. Being able to continue on as the person I was seemed utterly impossible. I saw no light at the end of the tunnel. There is a quote that says, "When a train goes through a tunnel and it gets dark, you don't throw out your ticket and jump off the train. You trust the engineer." I had no trust in the engineer. I had no trust in myself. I had no trust in my future.

CHAPTER 5

"Sometimes, all you can do is lie in bed and hope to fall asleep before you fall apart." William C. Hannan

My mother-in-law lost her husband when he had just turned 60. As previously mentioned, he retired early to help Pat get through the loss of his first wife. He went into the hospital for a hip replacement, and the day before he was to be discharged, a clot passed through his heart and killed him. Pat had just left and was getting in his car when his dad died. Dolly, Pat's mom, handled grief with so much poise and grace. I don't know how she did it. I would watch her surround herself with her kids and grandchildren. She put everything into her family. She would talk about her "hubby" with joy and never shed a tear, at least as far as I had ever witnessed. Their marriage wasn't without its hurdles either—what marriage isn't—but she never showed it. She never wore the badge of grief, and frankly, I am befuddled at how she did it.

I've been to several funerals in my years, where the spouse or relative gives the eulogy and can speak with so much composure, pulling in laughter, being so stoic. That is not in my make-up. I am a bumbling, babbling idiot when my emotions are in play. I just don't know how they do it. I wanted that strength. I wanted to have that courage. I wanted to be at that stage where I was on the other side of that dark tunnel.

My amazing grief counselor would say to me, "You've got to go through it to get through it." Which then triggered my dad's voice in my mind that would add, "The shortest distance between two points is a straight line," and here I am only able to scribble, desperately wanting to get out of the knot of grief.

I describe death as a thief in the night, and grief is its companion. Grief sticks around to remind you of what you lost. Just when you think you can go on, it rears its ugly head and says, "Not today." Death, on the other hand, pays no attention to your plans. It doesn't care how hard you worked to get where you are. It doesn't take into account your dreams. It has no regard for what it takes from you. Together, death and grief pilfer everything you ever had, and there isn't anything you can do about it.

About a month after I was robbed by this dynamic duo, my brother came from New York to help me paint my reminder away. It was a 48-hour marathon of painting, listening to oldies on the radio while we worked. Our day started around 7 AM and ended well after 9 PM. My only breaks were to prepare meals or to sit on a stool with a cold beer and admire our work. Ted is a beast when it comes to getting a job done. He paces himself and never stops; breaks don't last long. Together we accomplished what would normally take about four days to complete in two. We were quite the team. I think I logged 12,000 steps and 55 flights of stairs in just 16 hours without ever leaving my home. Whew!

As much as I was invested in having this change work, it did not. I still had flashbacks of that morning every time I walked into the bathroom. I changed the rugs, curtains, added new accents and wall decorations, and Pat is still laying on that floor today with the same distant stare. But those flashbacks didn't just happen at home—they followed me everywhere. During mass one morning, someone dropped the kneeler, and the clunk triggered an attack. I was walking in the bathroom and there he was again. I was starting CPR all over. I was fumbling to call 911. I was screaming at him to fight. The cracking of the ribs, the gurgling of the lungs—every detail as if it was just happening was clearly going through my mind.

They became so frequent, I never knew what was going to trigger this traumatic response. It could be a song on the radio, a commercial on TV, the sound of a car going by, a scent, a kid's scream, or the ringing of a bell. There was no rhyme or reason, no obvious connection to the events of that morning. They were, and still are, paralyzing. I heard a speaker once describe everybody as carrying an invisible backpack. These backpacks are filled with all of their worries, stresses, anxiety, losses, and the likes. Each of these trigger points carries a weight like a brick. He asked us to imagine the weight everybody in the room was carrying. I had a new brick added to my backpack: PTSD. It was chronic; it came with death and grief in a three pack.

To add to this cocktail of discontent, I wasn't sleeping, my appetite was all over the place. I would feel hungry, take a bite of something, and feel like I was going to throw up. I couldn't focus, didn't find pleasure in anything I did, and I was exhausted all the time. Grief evolved into depression. There is nothing like not having control over your feelings. Toss in a PTSD-triggered response, and you feel like everything you were is breaking apart. There is a Japanese art called Kintsugi, which means gold seams. When a piece of pottery is broken, the Japanese will put the pieces back together with gold because they still see the value of the object. The art celebrates the beauty of imperfection and reminds the artist that in our brokenness there is splendor. I wasn't feeling it—shattered with pieces missing was a better description.

I became apprehensive about leaving the house. Christine (my counselor) had me reminding myself that 'I was safe,' but I was waiting for that other shoe to drop. I had been in the basement of rock bottom before; I knew I could go lower. And this time, with my backpack so full, I didn't know if I would be able to make it back up. My Kintsugi was being held together by tape, not gold, and I was trying desperately to use it as it was intended, a container for my soul.

Let's continue on this theme of brokenness. Have you ever heard the Indian Proverb of the Cracked Pot? I'll paraphrase it here. A servant would get water for his master every day. He would carry two pots to the lake and fill them both up. One pot was cracked and by the time they reached home, it would only be half full. The pot felt bad for not being able to work effectively for the servant. But the servant showed the pot the path they had just walked up, and on one side, there were beautiful wildflowers growing, and on the other side, nothing but weeds. The servant said to the pot, "I used your brokenness, your flaw, to water the flowers that I am now able to pick and place on my master's table." I am that cracked pot, I don't know how many times I asked myself, what beauty can possibly come from my brokenness? I am still trying to figure that one out.

I just recently saw a Facebook post that says, "You need to be a little cracked for your light to shine through." I am fractured in so many places, you'll need to wear sunglasses. And that's how death, grief, and trauma leave you—in pieces. When your spirit and heart are so broken, the silence created from your loss is deafening. There is nothing that screams at you louder, and it makes it harder to fit those pieces back together. And no amount of gold will restore it to its original splendor.

You experience many firsts after losing your spouse. My 'first' was quickly approaching—his birthday without him. Pat was a March baby, and while his mother's side of the family had Lithuanian heritage, his dad's side of the family had Irish genealogy. If you were to ask Pat, he was 100% Irish. Because of this, he celebrated his birthday for the entire month of March. Christine asked me how I was going to celebrate it. I really didn't know. I wasn't ready to celebrate. I wasn't prepared to get over that hurdle and honestly, I was afraid I wasn't going to be able to clear it.

The cemetery where Pat's ashes were buried had a lot of restrictions. We were unable to add his name to the headstone, which had to be flush with the ground so they could mow. We weren't permitted to change the headstone because his dad served in the military and it was provided for his service. So the boys and I had a small marble memorial stone made up and we secretly placed it ourselves at the gravesite. We dug out an area for it, lined the bottom with sand and stones, leveled it off, and placed it even with the ground. That is how we spent his birthday. It was the last time I visited his grave. It brings me no comfort, only more flashbacks, and it gives grief permission to come out from hiding.

March was so empty. Even though I hung our sparkling shamrock on the door, wore green on Saint Patrick's Day, the one who filled the month up with laughter had been silenced, and there was no adjusting the volume.

April brought Easter, my birthday, and an unexpected side effect of PTSD. I had just gotten into my pajamas after Stephen and his girlfriend left from spending Easter Sunday with us. I had settled down to watch a comedy on TV, when all of a sudden I had tunnel vision. I had a small view of vision, with white light surrounding the dot of what I could see. My heart started racing, pounding so hard it felt like it was coming out of my chest, and breathing was difficult. I also felt a warm sensation move down from my head through both of my arms. Brian was upstairs in his room, and I tried to calmly call for him. All I could say was something's wrong. I used my Apple Watch this time to take my EKG, and I was having palpitations. Brian fumbled with his phone to call 911. He couldn't explain to them what was happening, so I took the phone. I had no chest pain, but at this point I was trembling and my heart was still racing. The first responders arrived, had me wired up to an EKG—no apparent heart attack. They saw the palpitations, but they appeared to be benign. Suggested Brian take me to the ER to be checked out, but they didn't feel it was bad, maybe dehydration or low potassium levels. If I wasn't feeling anxiety before, I am feeling it now. The unknowing, that horrible little voice that convinces you of all of the worst-case scenarios, was doing its thing in my mind. Why is this happening? Haven't I been through enough already? My grandfather died shortly after losing my grandmother; was I going to do the same thing? As I write this, I can feel my chest tightening, the underlayer is always there. I'll cut to the chase. This happened three more times in two and a half weeks. The first attack was a stress-induced cardiomyopathy, more commonly known as broken heart syndrome. Yes, it is real. It is associated with the increased cortisol your body produces as a result of long-term PTSD response. It reduces the potassium levels and mimics a heart attack. The other two were a minor recurrence of BHS, but categorized more as extreme panic attacks. I was now diagnosed with chronic PTSD, depression, and anxiety. As a result, I had stress-related heart palpitations. Grief is a bastard.

    I am three months into the loss of my husband, and nowhere near being the person I was before the thief stole everything from me. I am by default a ruminator—thanks mom. I come by it honestly; my mother was the same way. If I am not having PTSD-related flashbacks triggered by who knows what, my mind is set on replay, a form of quiet self-torture, playing over and over and over. I was a perfect storm for the anxiety attacks and the SIC. This is not me. This is not who I am. I have always been stronger than this. Why can't I pull my shit together and move on?

God, I hate this. Why did you take him from me? Why can't I move on? God, I am not as strong as you think I am. I can't do this. I hate it, I hate it, I hate it.

Well let's check how we are doing. Yup, we are still on the path of brokenness. Let me look behind me—nope, no flowers growing. How's that Kintsugi coming? Will Elmer's Glue work? Still looks pretty dark in this tunnel—oh look, another brick added to my backpack. Three months and the grips of grief are stifling.

As a result of the SIC, I have to do a stress test. Up until Pat's saddle clot, I was a walker—four miles at least four to five times a week. The stress test should be a breeze. *Insert thinking emoji here.* Let me preface some things for you. We are still in Covid protocol on doctor's visits. You have to be masked. I had a meniscectomy on my right knee and I am not supposed to run. I have Chronic PTSD. I am having benign palpitations. I just suddenly found my husband dead. I had to code him and you want this body to pass a stress test? Don't make me laugh. Do you know what delusional is? I failed. I don't mean I just failed. I failed with a high risk of having a heart attack. Would you have expected anything else?

Let's add to the growing list of specialists, a cardiologist that I am now seeing as a result of January 11, 2022. Not to mention, I am going through these health scares essentially alone. Are we having fun yet? The cardiologist does give me some comfort, and calls the results inconclusive because of the circumstances, but wants to do another test with an echocardiogram when my life settles back into some form of routine. I wonder when that will be? But remember, I told you I am a natural ruminator and that little voice in the back of my head is painting a bleak picture and I am buying into it. Who wouldn't at this point? I wish you knew the person I was before Pat died. This version that you are hearing about is not who I am or was.

I discovered that if I kept moving, the frequency of the heart palpitations would either stop or slow down. If I was sitting, I became one of those nervous nellies who always shake their leg and can't sit still. In a pinch, that was fine, but I needed to find something that was more productive. I purchased one of those portable ellipticals that you can sit in front of your chair and pedal away. At night, when I was watching TV, I would be pedaling for the entire show.

Without fail, when I laid my head on the pillow to go to sleep, they would start back up. When I had my initial broken heart syndrome attack, when I felt my chest tightening, I had started to listen to the Mary Undoer of Knots Novena I have on my Laudet app. The voice of the woman is soothing, her singing relaxed me, and I kept my focus on the repetition of the prayer. You've got to do what works. So after doing an hour or two of the elliptical, I would play the Novena as I was falling off to sleep to distract me from the palpitations. It also brought me a fraction of peace-of-mind because every night I went to bed, I wasn't sure I would be waking up the next day. That little voice (really needs a name) had me convinced I was going to die in my sleep. This is how Beth's dad died, and I knew it was in our family medical history.

At this point, I am also prescribed an antidepressant, taking horse pills of potassium, and a sleep aid. Better living through chemistry. I needed something more. I couldn't go to yoga classes because I didn't have anyone to watch Beth. You have to go through a training program, have a background check, and be approved by the agency of choice to be able to watch her. So I did the next best thing…YouTube. I discovered Yoga with Adrienne. I did contact my PCP to see if I was permitted to do yoga since there was still no confirmation on what was going on with my heart. Adrienne has a 15-minute mindfulness video that is perfect for reducing stress. Every morning I would get up, find my comfortable, quiet spot, and do the breathing and body scan with her. Within a few weeks, the palpitations stopped. Only to return when a former colleague and friend died from a massive clot while waiting in line at a CVS. Did I mention I have Chronic PTSD? Thank God for Adrienne and my Novena.

I would be remiss if I didn't mention, they did come back a third time and with a vengeance. My brother's mother-in-law died—God bless her at the age of 101—and that brought them on. They weren't the typical round of palpitations I was feeling before, so I went to the doctor, and my EKG came back with an irregularity in the T-wave, indicating a risk of ischemia.

Hadn't we just been down that path? After the results came back and I spoke with my regular doctor, he said he wasn't concerned. This was my new norm. New norm? There was nothing normal about it. It has been almost a year since my last run of palpitations. But just to note, we are only on Chapter 5—there is more in this area to come, of course there is.

CHAPTER 6

"Your absence walks through the door every single day." Helen Lyon

As I continue my year of firsts, we've now reached what would have been our 28th wedding anniversary. Let me ask you, sit with this for a minute, how do you undo the person you were for 27 years to fit the person you need to be without your husband? Who you were with him didn't happen overnight. Who you need to be now doesn't have time to ferment because life is continuing despite your world-ending loss.

The year before Pat's passing, we celebrated our 27th anniversary at a restaurant called Bube's. Yes, it is pronounced the way you are thinking. If you know me, I love history. I love old. I love a good ghost story and this had all three. Bube's was established in the 1700s as a beer brewery. A young, teen apprentice from Germany wanted to create a beer that would bring people from all over the world to enjoy it. He thought the key to good-tasting beer was to keep it at a constant temperature while it was fermenting. So he bought this piece of rocky land in Mt. Joy, PA, hulled out the rocks until he created catacombs to hold his wooden vats of beer. As the reputation for his beer grew, he built a hotel and bar for people to stay. The hotel and restaurant remained in the family for several generations and just in the past five or so years has changed hands. The catacombs are now an exclusive dining area, with casual dining on the upper level. To get to the catacombs is a minor adventure, walking over uneven ground that was the original rocky surface of the land, going down tapering stairs, squeezing your way through the narrow spacing of the original wooden vats, and being surrounded in stone over your head and under your feet. If you are claustrophobic, this is not the place for you. To add to the ambiance, the catacombs are said to be haunted by the ghost of Alois Bube's granddaughter, Pauline Engle. Best anniversary ever! The waitress shared the story of the catacombs and a little about the spirit that remains there. As we were eating, I heard this shuffling sound. The Catacombs have very low light, Christmas lights are strung on the top of the old barrels of beer and there are lit candles on each table. I looked at Pat with total thrill in my eyes—am I going to experience Pauline? It was when he asked me what my expression was for, it dawned on me he was setting me up for a tease, and that lightened our spirits for the rest of the evening. At that moment, he was the man I married, the man I loved so dearly, the person I felt so comfortable being with. This move was so good for us, restoring what the basement of hell had disrupted. It was wonderful to have us back.

How do I get past the anniversary of our wedding? What should I do? Do I need to do something? We moved to a Hallmark town. Literally, it has been used as a town setting in a couple of Hallmark movies. It is steeped in history, the main borough has maintained a lot of its historic charm and there is intent to keep it that way. The stores are very unique and the community is unlike any other, where kindness still exists. If there was a Mayberry, this is it. As we were sitting at the light in the center of town, I noticed a lamp in the window of a store. It had a mosaic globe as the lampshade on an antique brass pedestal. I commented to Pat, "I love that lamp," and he responded, "Get it." I shook it off, thinking it was probably too expensive and didn't give it much thought afterward. One day, months after Pat had passed away, Beth and I decided to stroll through town, to get out of the house and do something different. As I walked by the store front, the lamp was still there, and I could see the price tag—$84. I said to Beth, who didn't understand what I meant, "That's not as expensive as I thought it would be," and we continued our window shopping.

In the chaos of the morning when Pat died, I didn't realize his wallet got pushed under the bed. It wasn't until Ted and I painted that I found it, and then it took me a while to sit with it and open it. I found two things in it I didn't expect. One took my breath away and released a dam of tears; the other was a sign that my husband was still with me. Too many years to remember, I had cut a red heart out of construction paper and wrote on it, "My heart is perfect because… you are inside." I had put it in his lunch, and he kept it all these years. The second thing I found was $84. I bought the lamp. Godwinks. Those little glimpses that all you had together are not really gone. This would be a memorial for our anniversary. Thank you, my love.

Have you ever heard the superstition that if you find a coin or a feather, it is a sign that your deceased loved one is near? Pat collected dimes. I find dimes all the time—in parking lots, on grocery store floors, randomly in a shoe. I've started to keep a collection of all the times Pat was near.

There are so many times, not as many as I would like, that I catch a glimpse of my husband. One day while I was driving one of the back country roads to avoid traffic, I was thinking about Pat and how many times I had told him how much I loved it here. In the moments following that thought, an eagle soared overhead, the first I had seen since we moved here. My mind went back to that day at the mall when he promised our love would soar like an eagle. Soar my love, soar.

There are times when I am sitting alone, and I feel a hand on my shoulder. Or at night while I am sleeping, I wake up because it felt like someone sat on the foot of the bed. That one kind of creeped me out the first time it happened, but now it brings me comfort in the night. I think I hear his cough or clearing his throat, even an ooh or an aah at times, and I stop what I am doing to listen. Every day there is something that makes me think he's with me in some way. I can't wait for the day that those moments bring me smiles instead of tears.

I don't know if it is part of the grieving process or insanity, but there are so many times I think I am going to see him come through the front door and say this was all part of a bad joke. The disbelief that he is truly gone comes at you in waves. One of the tools my grief counselor provided me with is this Tear Drop Model of Grief by William Worden. It is the tasks of grief depicted in the form of a teardrop using the letters of the word T.E.A.R. as an acronym. When we lose someone we love, our first task, the letter T, is to accept the reality of that loss. We spend so much time in those initial days doing just that. Our mind is trying to discern what is real and what is not. The feeling that I described of thinking Pat will walk through that front door, when the reality is clearly he won't, is the task of T. The E of the model is experiencing the pain of that loss. In my journey through grief, I have learned that I revisit E quite often. There are always going to be times, moments, and events—something that triggers us and pulls us back to E.

Sharing with you the heart in his wallet brought me back to E. And if this provides any comfort to you, you visit E purely out of love—that's the one thing the thief cannot steal. The A is to adjust to a new life without the person. For me, I look at this as reinventing the wheel, and it will look differently to everyone based on their experiences. Currently, I am investing in that idea by making my home truly mine, not agreeing or settling on the decor because he didn't like a choice, but picking out what makes me feel truly comfortable. I am creating spaces where I feel safe. I am learning to budget. I've picked up a few side skills: lumberjack, carpenter, landscaper, plumber, electrician, auto mechanic, and I assembled an 11 x 11 pergola on our deck. When I finished and read the label, it said "3 person assembly required," and I said out loud, "or one 62-year-old woman" (and I did it in eight hours; the directions said two hours with three people). But whatever hat I am forced to wear, I am a work in progress, still getting used to walking on this tightrope. The final letter of the model is R. Reinvest in the new reality. I am still trying to figure that one out. I am only two and a half years into this journey. I think I am feeling more like the old me, but with new perspectives. I can say most of the time I am happy, and rebound faster when I am taken back to E. I don't know what my future looks like. Christine has asked me, but I don't have an answer. I am still very much stuck in that scribbling mess of lines, but grief was never described as a linear process.

* * *

In November of 2021, Pat and I gave ourselves a weekend away and booked a room at the historic Jim Thorpe Inn, in Jim Thorpe, PA, dubbed Little Switzerland. It's a quaint town, nestled in the nooks and crannies of the Pocono Mountains. If you have never been, I highly recommend it. The weather gave us a little challenge—it snowed early, a wet snow that melted quickly—but it stopped us from doing the walking tour of town. We both didn't trust Pat's knees on the wet sidewalks and the steep hills. So instead, we headed for a local casino and had a delicious and romantic steak dinner and lost a little money on the slot machines. That was our last weekend away together. This past March would have been his 70th birthday, so the boys and their girlfriends, along with some family members, met at Pat's favorite pub in Jim

Thorpe, Molly Maguires, and we celebrated him. When I passed the Inn, my heart sunk back to E. I don't think it is a reasonable expectation to think you'll ever get your life back to the way it was before death left its mark, but I do think we have it in us to make the best of where we are and be thankful for what we had.

I wish I could tell you it gets easier—it doesn't. We just learn how to distract ourselves better to move past the emptiness. Just recently, I was making something in the kitchen, Brian was watching TV in the den, and when I tasted it, I said to Bri, "Oh, your father would love this." He comes back when you least expect it. I don't want to get political here, but when I heard the news on the assassination attempt of Donald Trump, my first thought was, "I can't wait to tell Pat." These are the little things that will catch you and stab you, they'll make that lump in your throat choke you, and cause your eyes to water. It doesn't have to be anything in particular, but it is everything when you feel it, and the only positive I can say is we will rebound.

When I told you earlier that I have not gone back to the gravesite, I do not believe Pat is there. His ashes are, but I truly believe he is here with me. I feel him in this house. We may have only lived at this location a year and a half before he died, but this is where I feel him the most. I have his old recliner in my bedroom, his picture on the wall with the heart I gave him, a relic from Ireland, his mass card; and when I need to be near him, I go up and sit in that spot. I'll talk to him, yell at him, tell him about our boys, and ask him to keep an eye on them. It does bring me to some level of balance and makes me feel close to him. But I have to say, regardless of all of these signs, regardless of my amazing family and friends, I have never been more alone. I lost my confidant, the person I could share my most intimate fears with, the one who saw my flaws but loved me anyway. I lost my very best friend. I think I miss that the most.

***

Have you ever heard the analogy of the glass being half full or half empty? I have a different twist, a revelation in some respects. The glass is actually refillable, it is there that we need to focus. I had to stop writing this for a while, it was just so emotional, so at this point I am entering my fourth year of widowhood. But during my time away, I was working hard to focus on the positive. I may be a piece of Kintsugi by now, and I am refillable.

The trick to surviving is to continually tell yourself you are refillable. We are our own worst enemies at times, especially when we are hurting and vulnerable. We've got that negative voice in our minds that tells us we are half full, that we are broken, but ladies (and some gentlemen), we have experienced love, we've fought for it, we've honored it during some tough times, and because we have loved and were loved, we are refillable, love is the gold that will seal our cracks.

CHAPTER 7

"Grief is not a disorder, a disease or a sign of weakness. It is an emotional, physical and spiritual necessity, the price you pay for love. The only cure for grief is to grieve."

Earl Grollman

I broke my arm when I was a young girl. It took six weeks for the bone to heal and then another few weeks to rebuild the muscles back to their original strength. Depending on the injury, some healing processes can take longer. In most companies, you get one week off from work after the death of a loved one, and then you are expected to return and continue with life as if nothing happened. Neurological and psychological studies have confirmed that grief is not just an emotional process, but a physical one as well. The brain actually forms grief dendrites—little extensions of neurons, the part of your nervous system that transmits messages. It is a physical change, and once they have developed, you always have them. Different things stimulate the grief dendrites to become active and produce the grief response. As you move further away from the loss and cortisol levels start to normalize, the grief dendrites become less active, and the frequency and intensity of grief lessen. But it never fully goes away; it is a permanent physical change. If you are interested in that kind of thing, *The Grieving Brain*, by Mary Frances O'Connor is an interesting read.

    Our ancestors, depending on their culture, would take anywhere from six months to a year to recover from the loss of a spouse. Widows wore black for that time and did not leave their homes. Neighbors and family supported them, bringing food and whatever they needed. As society became more industrialized, employers and people stopped recognizing the toll of loss and cut back on the time given to grieve. As a result, today, most people have a difficult time dealing with grief. They are very uncomfortable with it. Often, they do not know what to say, and because of their own misunderstanding, they may distance themselves from the griever. I was blessed that most of the significant people in my life stuck with me through my ups and downs and never left my side. However, I am very aware of the awkwardness or discomfort in knowing what to say or how to act, especially when it comes to wanting to talk about the person you lost. I've had to remind myself that they've lost someone too—a friend, father, son, brother, uncle, coach, or colleague. Although it's the same person I am grieving, he had different roles in all of those lives, and these people will grieve in their own way over that loss.

Let me explain what this looks like for me. One of my challenges is that I am very empathetic. I internalize how people feel and end up putting their needs before my own. If I need to share my feelings and see they are uncomfortable, I hold it in and change the subject. As a result, those feelings get muted and fester until I can't handle them anymore. I'd rather have you think I have it all together and am happy, than let you know how heavy the backpack of bricks I am carrying really is and not project my feelings on to you.

As a teacher, I noticed that many students diagnosed with eating disorders, or who were cutters, or had depression, were often the happiest and most overachieving. What I didn't realize, until I had postpartum depression after Brian's birth, was that when you get into the privacy of your home without the distractions of work or school, the walls come crashing in. The old adage, 'don't judge a book by its cover,' holds a lot of truth here.

Being an empath by nature, I started to project my perceptions onto others. I figured they were tired of hearing me cry, tired of hearing me say how much I missed my husband, and tired of hearing my woes. Like the antidepressant commercial where people hide behind smiling faces, that became me, and is still me at times. I stifled myself, not because I was told to, but because I perceived myself as an annoyance. None of my group has ever said anything like this to me; they have freely let me process my grief, it was my own thinking. Conversely, I don't overburden them by talking about how I feel all the time, I hold those feelings close and closed, even to my most trusted supporters.

I follow the Sisterhood of Widows on Facebook, and I have read some heartbreaking stories where, just a month or so after the loss of their husbands, family members believe they should be over it and moving on with their lives. Not only have these women lost their spouses, but their support network is also breaking down. The reality is they will take months and years to heal, and the ignorance of others is only slowing their healing. Thankfully, I have never experienced this. I feel blessed by the people who have continued to support me as I go through this process.

With my heart scares, panic attacks, depression, and chronic PTSD, it is clear that healing is not just emotional but also physical. I do not know much about Chakras, but I understand that grief disrupts the balance in one or more of them. Chakra, meaning "wheel," has origins in ancient Buddhist teachings and relates to seven areas of your body where your energy is centered. When one Chakra is out of balance, it disrupts the energy in all the others. For me, the heart Chakra was affected, and it makes sense that I am experiencing issues in that area. We all carry our backpacks differently and manage based on our experiences and support network. Whatever your network looks like, which Chakra took the hit with your loss, or how you carry your burdens, know this—this moment is only a chapter in your life, and other chapters are waiting for you. This is not your whole book.

Grief is a major stressor, and I don't think that comes as a surprise to anyone. It not only takes an emotional and physical toll, but it also zaps the energy right out of you. You feel exhausted twenty-four/seven, and it takes more than a week to get over that. In my Foreword, I mentioned that family and friends, who genuinely mean well, often say, "Give it time and you will heal." I think that is the cruelest thing anyone could say to someone who is grieving. It provides false hope for something that is totally unachievable. You never truly heal from the loss of a spouse. You learn to cope, develop strategies, and adapt.

Losing a spouse is like having a limb amputated. You learn to live without it, but you have a constant reminder that it is not there and how you lost it. People with amputations can experience phantom pain, almost as though the limb was still there. People who grieve feel much the same way; their pain haunts them daily. There is no time limit to recover from your loss. No one should rush you or make you feel guilty for still grieving.

About three months after my husband's death, someone close to me said, "Joanne, give it time, you will heal and be back to your old self again." I looked at them and replied as politely as I could, "Please don't say that. I know you mean well, but this is not an injury you recover from. My job now is to learn how to live without him, to make new dreams, and manage on my own. This has nothing to do with healing, but everything to do with adapting."

Another phrase I couldn't stand to hear was, "I am sorry for your loss." I can't even stand to see it typed on this page; that's how much I resent it. I have some colorful expletives floating in my mind that I'd like to respond with, but I will refrain. "I am sorry for your loss" is something people say when they don't know what else to say. They are tossing a ball at you and hoping you will catch it. I am so aware of this that I no longer say 'I am sorry' about anything. Instead, I find other ways to express my condolences, like, "I know this is a difficult time for you, please know I will hold you and your family in my prayers." This statement is validating and lets them know they are not alone. Standing in the receiving line at the funeral, I was bombarded with a series of "sorry's," and each one made me cringe inside more than the last.

As I think this over, I also want to mention another irritant—the "let me know if you need anything" statement. If you know me, you know I rarely, if ever, ask for help. If I do, something must be really bad. First and foremost, in the weeks after Pat's loss, I didn't know what I needed. There isn't a handbook for widows and widowers that guides you through the steps after your spouse dies. You can't ask for help if you don't know what to ask for. One of my son's friends worked in the upper levels of a banking firm. He visited, and instead of asking me, "Mrs. Saunders (actually he said Mamma S), if you need help just let me know," he came armed with paperwork on how to file for my Spousal Social Security Support. I didn't know the first thing about it, but he wrote it all down and helped me navigate through the system.

One of my former colleagues lost her husband suddenly, a month before Pat passed away. Someone else I had worked with reached out to me, asking what she could do to help her. I recommended, instead of asking what she needs, it is better to offer something, offering to help grade papers, do grocery shopping, help with paperwork, and most importantly, follow through with it. Saying "just ask if you need anything," is an empty gesture.

I can't count the number of people who said, "Let me know if you need anything," and I never heard from them again. I attempted to take one friend up on their offer, only to be told they couldn't help. I was having what I thought was another stress-induced cardiomyopathy and asked if they could stay with Beth while Brian took me to the emergency room. They couldn't, so we brought her with us in her pajamas. To this day, I have a friend who tells me I need a girls' day out, and she comes and picks me up for fabric shopping and retail therapy. It's a day filled with laughter. She doesn't ask, she just does. We need those people who can easily step in without asking us to focus on our needs. Digging yourself out of the depths of grief isn't a one size fits all process. When you do not have the right people in your corner, it just makes it that much harder. It isn't fair to put expectations on the griever or on your support team. Expectations, when not fulfilled, create more disappointment. I've learned to limit my expectations.

I feel like I'm preaching to the choir—you know all of this. If you are reading this book because you lost your spouse, I'm certain you've felt the same way. What I need you to know is that you are not crazy; you are safe, and honey, you do you. Whatever you need to do to get beyond this miserable place, do it, even if it means stepping on a few toes along the way. You can always say what you need to say politely. Once the message is delivered, it's no longer yours to worry about. You have to take care of yourself, for as long as it takes. As a people pleaser, this was one of the hardest steps for me.

If you can, find your person. By that, I mean the one person who will be there for you even in your worst moments. When my husband passed, a dear friend called or texted me every day for the first year, just to check in, say hello, and offer a safe shoulder to grieve on. She validated my feelings. She never tried to fix me; she would listen and, as she described it, she was a vessel. Within the same year that I lost Pat, she lost her daughter to a drug overdose. Today, we grieve together and are vessels for each other. Her daughter's memorial service has been the only service I have been able to attend since Pat's passing. I can't risk being triggered by something that is being said.

* * *

With the year of firsts behind me, it was time to enter the second year of grief. I was told by several people that the second year is worse than the first. Now that you've managed to survive the first year, people expect you to be okay and have little tolerance for your pity party. They don't want to hear it anymore. As I mentioned before, people are uncomfortable with someone who is grieving. We have removed the culture of thinking and are forced to move on before we are even ready. No matter how the world views the griever, this pales in comparison to the realization that Pat was not coming back. I had to pull up those big girl panties and suck it up buttercup—my knight in shining armor was not coming back to save the day. I was on my own.

So let's try out this new, floundering solo act. I know they tell you not to make any big decisions the first year, but there were some things I felt were unavoidable. With Brian commuting to college, he needed a more dependable car. Pat had just had ours repainted and fully serviced, and it was covered under an extended warranty that included towing and emergency services. I had the will probated and used some of that money to buy myself a new car. We sold Brian's old hand-me-down from his grandmother, and he got mine. This would give me peace of mind when he was on the road and the security of traveling to my family, who were four hours away. This was a big step—my first independent decision. The one thing I felt I needed above anything else was security, and it needed to be done. There was also a secondary reason—I was determined not to let grief control me. My intent for the second year was to prove them all wrong—it would not be harder than the first.

Harder is relative, I think I said that before. It's a different type of struggle. Taxes killed me. Even though I had the wherewithal to set aside money just for taxes, it wasn't enough. Social security took back over $8,000 of my survivor's benefits. I suddenly became $23,000 in the hole. My wages for Beth's care are fixed, and what I owed was a third of my earnings. I didn't have the wherewithal to anticipate this, and am still struggling to get those bills down. If I want something for the house, I buy second-hand. I have found a great auction site that I make bids on, the proceeds go to the family in transition. I know a lot more than I want to about transition.

But back to the problem—this is the crazy thing about Social Security (SS). They can go right into your bank account and take what they want. So, when I went to pay bills, things were bouncing left and right. I spent hours on the phone, trying to navigate the system. It doesn't matter the hand life dealt you—they are holding the deck of cards and will deal what they like. Some had sympathy and worked with me, while others were ice cold. I put my electricity and gas on budget plans, reduced my TV and Wi-Fi bill by getting a different bundle, and didn't need the sports stations, as I could stream the shows I usually watch. I bundled my homeowners and auto insurance, and got a lower rate health insurance. By the way, I pay more now that Pat is gone. It was less when he was alive. Does that make any sense? Your income is less, so they charge you more. Being my own bookkeeper wasn't the problem—I had done this before I was married—but Social Security and taxes screwed me over. Finances added another brick to that already full backpack.

What also got to me was that intense feeling of being alone. I had no one to bounce my concerns off of. Don't get me wrong, my friends and family were always there, but I didn't have Pat, and my need for him became exponential.

Pat leveled me, kept me in balance, made me feel accomplished, and knew me so well that he could pull me off the ledge when I was feeling overwhelmed. I was solo, and now I had to do that all on my own. This kind of alone is far different from sitting in your house by yourself. It's all on your shoulders; no one else can do it for you. Have you ever tried to pay a bill online? You have to jump through so many hoops to make a payment. Think about that—if you don't have the correct information, you aren't allowed to give them money. Sounds counterintuitive, right? This is what this type of alone feels like, trying to do the right thing but not having what you need to do it.

Twenty-seven years with a person changes you. You depend on each other to fill your weaknesses, and the minute you lose your partner, you lose what held you together. I am oddly grateful that Pat died after we moved here because I would have lost everything if we were still living where we were. I am also thankful for my time in the basement of rock bottom, as it gave me the experience I needed to navigate all of this. Over these two and a half years, I have utilized skills that I never fully understood why I had to learn, but at some point, you will.

Remember when I said my counselor told me you had to go through it to get through it? The only way to get past grief is to allow yourself to grieve, and you do that for however long it takes. If you break a limb, you have to go through rehab until you regain the use you had before. Grieving is your rehab—take as long as you need and watch out for those E's.

NOTE As I reread this for editing purposes, I notice that some chapters flow coherently, while others seem to jump around. I've decided to leave them that way because they illustrate the true picture of grieving. There are moments when you have it all together, and everything flows nicely, and then there are times when you are all over the place, just trying to control what you can, fumbling to hold it all together. It's the perfect example of what this journey looks like and a reminder to look for the calm in the chaos.

CHAPTER 8

It is always important to know when something has reached its end. Closing circles, shutting doors, finishing chapters, it doesn't matter what we call it; what matters is to leave in the past those moments in life that are over."

Paulo Coelho

Midway through the second year of my loss, which I'll refer to as Life After Pat (LAP), I hit a brick wall. I was sharing with my brother the hopelessness I had been feeling. There was no happiness in my life. I was going through the motions, doing all the right things, but I was so lost I couldn't see beyond the day I was currently in. I commented that I wasn't suicidal, but if God wanted to take me now, I wouldn't fight. I did, in fact, want to die, but not by my own hands. I described it this way: I felt like I was swimming underwater, trying desperately to come up for air, and someone or something was always there to push me back under. I was tired of trying to catch my breath, tired of treading water, tired of the constant fight.

I mentioned before that when I found my new parish, I offered my assistance in their Kairos Retreat. Kairos, if I can advertise for a moment, is an amazing four-day discovery of faith retreat offered to high school teens. The word 'Kairos' means God's Time. A lot of what happens at the retreat is kept under a veil of secrecy because the unknowing can provoke a deeper reaction, almost like tasting food with a blindfold on brings out more of the flavors. It's an absolutely amazing time for the retreatants, teen leadership team, and adults. The priest led what I call a mindwalk, where you close your eyes and he descriptively guides you through imagining a place. He had us mentally walking a trail, and at the end, a man in white stood. When the man turned around, you were supposed to be face-to-face with Jesus. I could not see His face. It was blackened out. This upset me and I didn't understand why I couldn't see the face of Jesus. When we had a moment, I shared my image with Father. To him it was obvious, my trust and faith was blocked.

My faith journey was awakened and ignited during my college years. Since then, I have relied heavily on it to get me through the good and the bad seasons of my life. When we had our stent in the basement of rock bottom, I went to my favorite walking trail, headed down one of the paths that were less traversed, stood under the canopy of trees, held my hands up to the sky, my fists unclenched and cried "God I can't do this anymore. I am not an Isrealite, I don't have all of those years to wander in the desert. Please God help us." Tears were streaming down my face, I was trembling. I looked down at my feet and there was a blue chicory flower trying to push its way up through the cracks in the pavement. My tears turned into laughter. At that moment I felt a weight being lifted off of my shoulders and I heard God's answer through that flower, "Beautiful things can grow in the most impossible places." Not long after, we resolved our financial problems and bought our new home free and clear.

Here I am, a year and a half after my loss, and I have no faith to fall back on. I was angry at God. I couldn't understand why He would bring us here and then take Pat away. I was going through an emotional faith struggle. One part of me knew I should be grateful for the time we had here; Pat was able to see how happy I was, and we were able to repair some of what was broken between us. But a bigger part of me was ripped away. It was obvious to me why I could not see Jesus' face on the mindwalk, but still shocking nonetheless. I can't say that I stopped praying, but I was just going through the motions; my heart wasn't in it. Many of my prayers started with, "God, I don't even know why I ask; You're going to do Your own thing, but…" With that spiritual void, I felt hopeless. Without Pat, I saw no future.7

Around this same time, my sister-in-law called. She and her daughter had gone to a psychic who mentioned that Pat was one of the biggest presences in the room. That was exactly his character; he had a magnanimous presence. Now don't quote me on this, I will deny it, but I was taught to believe it is a cardinal sin to go to a psychic—it's against church teachings, and its roots are connected to Satan, at least that is my understanding. Their session with the psychic intrigued me. He knew things he could not have possibly known, things I hadn't shared with Debbie.

Here are some of the things that surprised me. I had given Stephen my engagement ring and wedding band so he could propose to his girlfriend. The psychic mentioned that Pat was happy about the rings. Deb did not understand what that meant, as we hadn't announced the upcoming engagement or my decision to give them the rings. He brought up something about a picture at the funeral, saying he didn't like the one we chose. It's the one I have hanging in my bedroom now. There was mention of a hat and why did Joanne leave it with her brother. I was supposed to take a group of students to the Galapagos Islands before Covid hit. Pat bought me a sunproof straw hat for that trip, and I use it at my brother's when we are out fishing. There were specific things that the psychic shared that he had no way of possibly knowing. This festered in me for months. The desire of seeing a medium myself was nagging at me. And given where my faith stood, I didn't care if I violated church law—God would just have to understand, He put me here.

***

Do you believe God sends people to us, strangers to act as His angels or messengers on Earth? I do. Just recently, I had another meniscectomy, this time on my left knee. I wish I could say I was running a 5K marathon and that's how I injured it, but I was walking into the grocery store when I felt three pops. It was a complex tear, with a piece lodged between my tibia and femur. I was one week post-surgery. I had to pay my local taxes, and since they were late, I had to take them physically to the tax office. I was given the wrong location and wound up walking seven city blocks on a hot and humid day, only to be told they would only accept cash or I could complete it online. I was tired, my knee was throbbing, I didn't feel like cooking dinner afterwards, so Beth and I headed to our favorite Village Farm Market to get the best hoagies in town. When I went to pay for the sandwiches, my debit card was declined. The Mennonite clerk ran the card again. I was getting embarrassed. I said to her, "Everything I have tried to do today has been a struggle and I am trying to figure out what I am supposed to be learning from all of this." The young girl sheepishly answered, "Patience?" No, I don't think that was it. I asked her to void the transaction and give me a minute to call the bank. There was no reason the card should be declining; I could have paid for every order that was being placed at the market and then some. When I walked back in, I was surprised to find that the woman after me had paid my entire bill. I broke down in tears and cried all the way home. At that moment, I knew God was watching what I was going through and sent me an angel to let me know He was with me. It was the first time in a while, I felt Him there with me.

So, with that story under your belt, maybe you can understand a little of what I am about to share. My grief counselor, also a practicing Catholic at the same church I attend, told me about a psychic some of her clients have gone to and how they were surprised at the accuracy of her readings. She had told me this maybe a year into our sessions. After hearing about Debbie's experience, I inquired again and found out her name and contact information, and signed up for an hour session. I don't recommend this for everybody, but for me, she was another angel. What she shared with me renewed my faith, restored my trust in God, and emptied that backpack of bricks. I am back. I am excited about life, I am happy, and I know with God, all things are possible, and we make an awesome team.

You are probably chomping at the bit to hear what she said. Before I tell you, let me say it was not one thing or one person, but a collective image that she was able to channel and create. You also need to know that I went in with what I thought was a healthy skepticism and the intention of not answering any questions that could lead her to say anything or give her any clues. My father was the first presence to come up. I never thought I was smart enough for my dad's standards. He was an excellent provider, but I always felt my brothers were the "do-no-wrong" type for him. Francine looked at me, took a deep breath, and with a little choke in her throat said, "He wants you to know he has always been proud of you." That's it—the first revelation—and I am bawling my eyeballs out. "He is always with you," she added. Those Facebook quizzes have told me the same thing, so she must be right (I hope that made you laugh). "He wants you to know he is grateful to you and your brothers for taking such good care of them when they were unable to care for themselves." I was blubbering, ugly sobbing—where is this coming from? "Your dad loved to play cards, and he is quite the socialite. He can easily talk with anyone." Sunday afternoon Pinochle parties with my grandparents were his favorite, and there wasn't a stranger he would pass without asking, "Where are you from?" It was his conversation starter.

My mom was next on deck. She needed me to know she was with her father, and before she could pass over into heaven, she had to make amends with him, and he had to make amends with her. My mom hated her dad. When he died, she didn't attend his funeral, never—or rarely—spoke about him, and was reluctant to explain her anger towards him. I was taken aback by this revelation. How does she know this? There are only a handful of family members who know this, and half of them are dead. It's definitely not on a social media post somewhere.

Beth's father was there. He wanted to thank me for taking care of his daughter. He needed me to know that there will come a day when Beth will have to be sent elsewhere, and that will be okay. I am going to skip something here and bring it up when I mention Pat, but he was glad we had each other.

It wasn't over. She told me I was currently dealing with some health issues and felt it was heart-related. The doctor would tell me that this is my new norm. The following week after my EKG, I saw my primary care doctor. His exact words were, "Joanne, this is your new norm; there is nothing to worry about."

It was then Pat's turn. He had been present the whole time but waiting. She was holding a small urn with his ashes in it, one that both Stephen and Brian wanted. She described Pat, and other than weight, she was spot on. She told me she needed to describe to me the process he went through after he died, saying it is the process we all go through. She explained that our souls know each other before we come down to Earth. We sit at a table with God, and He shows us several paths our mortal life can take, and we choose the path. Pat and I chose to be on the same path together, and he knew when his journey with me would end. In fact, he was allowed a little longer and didn't die when he should have. Was that when he had the saddle clot in November, I thought to myself?

She said we were truly soulmates and would be together again. The souls of Beth and I had been very close, and she too chose to be on the same path and decided to come in a way where she could be of help to me. Francine said that when Pat died, he was confused. He saw me trying to revive him, but he had to pass through a door and sit at a table to reconcile his life. He had no regrets he hadn't already sought forgiveness for, but he did regret having to leave me so soon. It was all his fault. Then she said something to me that would change everything: "He wants you to know you are more purely and profoundly loved now than he was ever able to love you on Earth. There is nothing in the way of his love for you—no health issues, no depression, no earthly worries." That was it. That is what I needed to hear, and that is what I carry with me today.

You can say that I sinned, that going to the psychic was wrong, but as I have said throughout this book several times, God's hand has been in everything and He was talking to me through Francine. I have never been more devout in my Christian faith as I am today. If she was evil, Satan's plan backfired. If I tell you God sends us the most unlikely angels at unexpected times, you can believe He does and will.

CHAPTER 9

"An Apache scout told me once that when you love somebody, you trade souls with them. They get a piece of yours, and you get a piece of theirs. But when your love dies...a little piece of you dies with them, that's why it hurts so bad. But that little piece of him is still inside you. And he can use your eyes to see the world."
Shea Brennan 1883 (Yellowstone)

People see me as always happy. If you were to ask them, they'd say I have handled Pat's passing magnificently. My brothers will tell you how proud they are of how far I've come, amazed by my resilience. They are learning a lot from my journey. My sons, who have friends that have lost parents, have also commented on how I have handled all of this in comparison. Friends will tell you they have seen a change in me—a change of strength and character. But I will tell you that is not the way I see myself. I wish I could see that person through their eyes. I feel like a mess and like a con-artist; I can make it look like I am okay when inside I am doing all I can to hold it together. It is exhausting, to say the least, to make it through the day with grief as your sidekick.

Grief has a remarkable grip on you. It controls you, changes the way you see the world, and impacts how you respond. It is almost like an out-of-body experience—you watch yourself or hear yourself say or do something and think, was that really you? I have thought of myself as a very accepting person, but life with grief has made me so intolerant. I rarely watch the news. I check the weather and look at the headlines. I read through social media posts and see so much hate. Case in point: someone new to the community posted that they had moved here from New Jersey and were wondering where they could get good pizza. A commenter posted "move back to Jersey" as his answer. Why do we have to be so callous? I used to be able to filter all of this through my husband, but death and grief stole that outlet from me. I do admittedly spend a lot of time on social media, looking for positivity, gratitude, and profound posts. I follow the Sisterhood of Widows, which I wasn't able to do early on, but I can now.

I want to take you back to the week before Pat died. Grab your Kleenex. I think you will agree, we had a lot of obstacles during our married years. We navigated through some moments that really should have separated us—many that I have not mentioned here. Because we had been friends before anything else, we cleared the hurdles that were meant to break us. Our sons were young adults and able to be on their own, and our move to the new house and town was supposed to be our starting over moment. Covid added a little wrench to those plans, but we worked around that the best we could.

I was struggling with some low libido levels due to menopause. It was hard for Pat to understand my lack of interest in that area. We had seen the doctor together, tried some medications he recommended, some of which had side effects that were difficult to get used to. It became an uncomfortable subject to discuss—I felt like I was failing him, and he felt like I was slipping away from him. This was what we were trying to work through, together.

Pat died on a Tuesday, just to provide a timeline. Sunday morning, I surprised him by slipping into the shower with him. I had music playing in the background, and we had a very touching, romantic moment. He apologized for not loving me the way he should have through the tough times and promised me he would make sure that never happened again. He promised to take care of himself so we could start enjoying our plans together. He told me how much he loved me, how he was proud of me, thanked me for giving him two beautiful sons, and we just held each other tight. I have always liked how my head nestled into the dip of his chest—it was a perfect fit. Sometimes I get into the shower and swear I can still feel him holding me like he did that day. I close my eyes and try to remember every moment, every touch, every word. But now I wonder, looking back, did he know he was saying goodbye? Did he sense something was wrong then?

Monday morning, as we were getting ready for the day, I brought the speaker into the bedroom, turned on my iTunes, and played "Nobody But You" by Blake Shelton and Gwen Stefani, the song I quoted in Chapter 3. We danced, held each other close. When the line that says, "I don't want to live without you, I don't even want to breathe" came up, I spoke those words to him (nobody wants to hear me sing; he would have divorced me on the spot!). The next song I had set to play was "Just to Hear You Say That You Love Me" by Faith Hill and Tim McGraw. The next day, he was gone...

I gave the biggest fight of my life to save him. I lifted a 237 lb man off the seat he was on, laid him on the floor, and did everything possible to pull him back into my world. I was in a fight with God to bring him back to me, and I gave it everything I had in me—a piece of me left with him that day. I believe we are soulmates. From the moment Maria dared me, our future together was set in motion. I don't know how else to explain how we held it together and how we were able to come back to each other.

Somewhere in the chaos of the aftermath, I snuck away and listened to those songs, trying to regain the feeling, the touch, the love, and cried a bucket load of tears. Those two days are what I hold on to; they are the only real memories I allow myself to spend time with. I may talk about things we did together, but these two moments are mine and mine alone.

I still go into the shower, sit on the floor while the water is running, and just cry. It's one of the most cathartic things I do. I wish I could say I can enter my bathroom today without seeing him there with that empty gaze in his eyes, but the best I can say is that for a while now, the trigger of flashbacks it produced has subsided.

***

I have unspoken hopes that until this moment, I have never shared. When I look at our sons, I hope Pat sees them through my eyes, and when he does, that he's just as proud. I know in heaven there isn't time like we know it here on Earth; love is abundant, there is no pain or suffering. But will you remember to check in? They still need their father. And my biggest hope is that you can see and feel my love and how much I still need you with me.

Today, as I am writing this, I am eleven months into my third year without him. Funny how you count the years of death like you do with a child, "oh, he's 27 months old." I am 38 months in widow time and it seems like a lifetime. This year I have focused on myself. I am no longer trying to reinvent the wheel.

CHAPTER 10

"One day we will remember how lucky we were to have known their love, with wonder, not grief"

Elizabeth Postel

Why do people subject themselves to physical and emotional pain? As a former educator of teens, I struggled to relate to the young teen who was a cutter. I couldn't understand why they would put gashes on their thighs and stomach, inflicting pain and causing scars. However, after losing my husband, I began to see things more clearly.

Our youngest son, Brian, is quite the comedian. I've often remarked that I see glimpses of Robin Williams' sense of humor in him. The Christmas before Pat died, Beth gifted Brian a onesie lounging suit. Brian is always cold, so he immediately put it on. With Mariah Carey's "All I Want for Christmas" playing in the background, he danced through the kitchen in his blue onesie, pillow-stuffed belly and all, moving like the Philly Phanatic. I quickly pulled out my phone and recorded the moment. We were all laughing, cheering, and getting into the action.

That first Christmas without Pat, I decided to go through my videos—a task I had avoided until then—and came across this now-family-classic video. Hearing Pat's voice in the background for the first time in almost a year was like being punched in the stomach. The overwhelming nausea, the gut-wrenching wail of grief, and the monsoon of tears that followed don't even come close to describing my reaction. The emotional pain of hearing his voice was unbearable, yet I played it over and over again. Each time, I tortured myself, feeling the pain made him real, made us real, made everything real. I finally understood, and while I wasn't creating physical scars, I was etching emotional ones.

Christmas is, in itself, a difficult time for people who have lost loved ones. There is an empty desire to have them with us, sharing in the love and laughter of the season. Our minds can be very cruel to us as we ruminate on past Christmases with them and then focus on not having them here. I used the word 'empty,' but in reality, it's a void or more like a vacuum that just sucks everything out of you. To compensate, some will try to create new traditions to remember loved ones who have passed away, and that is exactly what I did. But nothing really fills the sinkhole that is left.

For me, Pat's death took my Santa Claus away. Literally. I needed something to commemorate that time in our lives, so I bought a Lenox Santa in his memory. That Santa goes on the mantle of the fireplace every year. I also bought a crystal North Star to hang near the top of the Christmas tree. Like that crystal eagle, it was a symbol of my husband being my 'true north.' Through all of our ups and downs, he balanced me—we balanced each other. It is a reminder of that balance. When it is not hanging on the tree, it is hanging in my bedroom window. I wake up to it and go to sleep with it every day. I saved some of his flannel shirts. I wear them when I want to feel his arms around me. I still have his cologne, which I sparingly spray. All of these and more are the ways I keep him with me through every season.

I would be lying to you if I said the holidays get easier. In reality, you are still traversing the same rough waters, but you've hewn the skills it takes to navigate them. This year, our third Christmas without our personal Santa, we decided to open the emotional gifts on Christmas Eve. That left Christmas open for laughter. It worked for us and was closer to the Christmases we have known.

Here I am on the eve of the next anniversary of the greatest loss of my life. This year marks the start of the fourth year without my love. I have some good news to share: I was taken off my antidepressants, no more palpitations, and my stress and anxiety evaluations have been within normal ranges. I now see my grief counselor once a month instead of every other week. When I look back at what I did to get here, I can't believe I made it with any piece of mind left. The past two months have been different. Handling the visits back to 'E' without taking Zoloft has been a challenge, but I have worked through them, and I no longer get stuck there. I have strategies in place and goals I am working towards.

This year is about renewal—getting back on track, taking care of unfinished business and finances, taking care of me, and setting boundaries. The loss of a spouse is something you will always carry with you. It is different from other losses because your role in it is different. You never really "get over it"; it is now a part of the tapestry of who you are. I once described to a friend that the people we meet are like adding color to a painter's palette. Some blend together and make beautiful new colors, while others darken and can dull, even diminish the color, or they can make other colors stand out. That is what loss does. It adds another color to the palette—a color that will overpower the brightest hues and will pull out hues that once just blended in, and that new shade is you.

***

So what is next? People who have fallen into the grips of substance abuse and are working their way out learn that they are always in recovery mode. They have to be vigilant not to fall back into the same patterns and habits that got them stuck in the first place. Grief has to be treated with the same vigilance. It's always going to be with the widow or widower, even if they find new love and remarry. I first experienced this with Pat. When we started dating, Barbara was still very much a part of his tapestry, that was never going to change. He brought a lot of the emotion and grieving into our relationship. To some, this may be a threatening thought, but for me, I saw it as an example of how deeply he was capable of loving. It goes back to that refillable glass—it is a matter of perception. In order for our relationship to grow, I had to accept that it was a part of who he was. At that time, I could never understand it in the way I do now. It took a remarkable amount of courage and energy for him to move on into a new relationship and open himself to loving again. Because I understood this, I did everything to include Barbara in our journey together. I respected the love they shared.

Two and a half years ago, I answered a Facebook post to rescue a young, pregnant kitten. The woman caring for the stray had lost her first husband and remarried. I was drawn to her, and we immediately became friends. Despite our short friendship, we've shared many tears. She validates my recovery process and makes me feel like I still have some sanity left. Like Pat, she has remarkably and bravely found someone to love while still honoring what she shared with her late husband. Her friendship and marriage have provided me with hope that there's more in store for me. I believe she was heaven sent, placed here to help me move forward.

I hope you have people in your corner who are being your vessel and providing you with the support you need. The situation that has been thrust upon you is not for the meek of heart and is better faced when you have a network of angels helping you adapt. I am greatly and uniquely blessed by my people. They have allowed me to crumble without judgment, given me a lift up, stepped in when I couldn't step up for myself, listened even when I repeated the same thing for the hundredth time, provided distractions, and believed in me when I couldn't believe in myself.

Our journey as widows is unlike anything we have walked before, and those angels help make the hike easier.

If by chance you are reading this and your network is dysfunctional, find new people. Don't be afraid to leave behind those who cannot be there for you. They are not your group; they will keep you stuck in the fog of grief, and you don't need that. Sometimes we have to muster all the energy we can to self-advocate. There will be some who will intentionally and unintentionally undermine your efforts. I will say it again: they are not your people.

When Pat died, I was new to our community. My friends and family were over an hour away. COVID had impacted our ability to develop new friendships, and we felt isolated even in our church community. So when he passed away, I was in a strange and unknown place, critically wounded, with no clue who to reach out to locally. I described earlier the feeling of being alone in a room full of people; I was alone in a town where I knew no one, and there was no returning home. So when I say find new people, I've done just that.

There are some quotes I am reminded of as I write this: "You become who you surround yourself with," attributed to Rachel Hollis, and "You are the average of the five people you surround yourself with the most," often attributed to Jim Rohn. These quotes highlight that the people you choose to interact with will impact and influence your life and choices. So choose wisely.

CHAPTER 11

"Our boundaries define our personal space-and we need to be sovereign there in order to be able to step into our full power and potential."

Jessica Moore

A friend of mine was going through a personal struggle and needed me to be her sounding board. I am inclined to be a Florence Nightingale, rushing in to save the day. After hearing her concerns, I offered a possible solution, a remedy for her to take as needed. Her response surprised me, "I am not broken; you do not have to fix me!"

This made a couple of things apparent. First, sometimes people do not need you to respond—they just need someone to listen without judgment. This is a critical part of the healing process and being mindfully present for the person who trusts you to hold their place. Second, my friend perceived that I thought she was broken and needed fixing.

I gleaned two things from this experience. One, our best intentions are not always received the way we envision. Two, brokenness was somehow seen as a bad thing. Let me address the second point before I go on. We are all broken; we've talked about this before. We are like cracked pots, but it is in our brokenness that the light we hold inside can finally shine through. There is no shame in being broken and needing to be fixed. Scars are reminders of lessons we have learned; they are our badges of courage and a sign of strength.

The third takeaway, which will be the basis of this chapter, is that my friend was setting a clear boundary. She was establishing what she needed and firmly held her ground.

Let me put my teacher's hat on for a moment. Boundaries are limits or guidelines that define what is acceptable and what is not in a given situation. For those of us who are grieving the loss of our significant other, boundaries are especially important. We have well-intentioned friends and family rushing in to "fix" us. Our Florence Nightingales come in all shapes and forms, with different life experiences they feel can help us get back on our feet. This is how some people heal themselves after their loss. They've lost someone too in this whole mess—the same person, but that person played a different role in their lives: father, brother, cousin, friend, colleague, etc. By trying to help you, they are reaping the benefit of helping themselves process the loss. I know I forgot that in the first hours and days after losing Pat. In those moments, it was all about me.

In the birth of this trauma—and it is a trauma—we need these people to help us navigate our way. But sometimes they get too comfortable telling us what to do and how we should feel, continuing this behavior in the weeks, months, and years later. This is where you use the tool of boundaries. I admit, it can be pretty scary at first. I am not of the mindset to tell people what they can or cannot do. I fear alienating those that I need. Maybe you can relate to that way of thinking. I find myself justifying their actions: "Oh, they mean well," and negating my own feelings. The first time I set a boundary, I was a nervous wreck, imagining everything that could go wrong. I was surprised to find out, sometime later, they were very proud of me for standing up for myself and validated the strength it took to do so.

What I would like to do here is focus on my immediate family and the boundaries that I have had to set. I must preface this by saying that I have to do what best serves my needs, just as you will have to adjust to what best serves yours. I have mentioned before, grieving is not 'one size fits all'.

It always amazes me when I look at my two sons and see how they handle things today, knowing they were raised with the same set of values, beliefs, and moral compass. Yet, each one is uniquely their own individual, and sometimes I wonder, "Where did they come from? I didn't teach them that!" They are both young adults, 25 and 28, with experiences in their youth that have shaped their perspectives. Stephen, the oldest, was always the one who let things roll off his back, much like water on a duck's feathers. Brian, on the other hand, was high-strung; he held everything in and, like his mother, ruminated on everything. The loss of their father meant different things to each of them.

A brief background on the relationships these two young men had with their father will help set the stage for a better understanding of the need for boundaries. Stephen was very athletic, like his dad. His coordination was instant—he was walking at nine months old. He and his father enjoyed talking about sports and could relate to each other on many different levels. Brian can be summed up simply by saying, 'I cloned my husband'. While not as coordinated at first—he walked at 10 months—he had different athletic interests and had to work at his skills. Personality-wise, he was just like his dad. You know what they say about how you dislike what you see in others because you can see it in yourself? That was Pat and Brian. They were at odds with each other early on.

Stephen could always easily talk with his father; Brian could not. Let's admit, Pat was not always the easiest man to talk with. I am not trying to make excuses—it's the simple truth. You can ask many people who knew him; he could be rough. Brian and Pat were in the process of repairing a fractured relationship when his dad died. There was a lot of unfinished reconciliation that remained. Stephen didn't answer a call from his dad the day before because he knew he could easily catch up at another time. That became a boulder in his personal invisible backpack.

You have to imagine, on the morning I found my husband unresponsive, I had just fought for his life, performed CPR and coded him. I am just a teacher, not a medical professional, with only CPR training and never having used it until that day, so this was very traumatic to my psyche. Equally heart-wrenching was seeing our sons sitting on the bathroom floor with the lifeless body of their father. You cannot unsee that. And as PTSD would have it, I have that vision more regularly than I would care to. That morning changed all of us and quickly thrust the boys into parenting roles. I became old and less capable in their minds as a result. They switched from sons to guardians of their mother; it was an immediate transition. Let me clear the air: Pat was seven years older than me. I was 61 when he died, a very young, agile 61 years old. I was just out paintballing with my sons and brother, hiking the rainforest in Costa Rica with a group of my students and ziplining the Monteverde Cloud Forest not too long before all of this, so I was far from old and decrepit.

    Remember when I said that well-intentioned, loving people will try to help as part of their healing process? This was the path our sons were on. Brian transferred colleges so he could live at home and help me out. Stephen was living in the Philadelphia area but made the trek out at least every other week until softball season started, or his girlfriend got tired of him leaving—I'm not sure which came first. Instead of working with me, they began telling me what I could or should do and instructing me on what I needed to do. They were also harsh, at times, in the way they spoke to me. This is when I set my first boundary.

The next time we were together, I sat them down and started by saying how much I loved and appreciated them. I validated that their loss was different from mine—losing a dad is far different from losing a spouse—but I acknowledged that we were mourning the loss of the same person. In the workshops I had taken over the years that involved conflict resolution, I learned it was always better to establish common ground and validate feelings. Then I set my boundary.
"I need you two to know, I will always be your mom; that will never change. But I also need you to know that I am also Joanne, and Joanne has feelings, concerns, and fears. You cannot talk to Joanne the way you do your mom." Cha-ching, the lightbulbs went

on. You could see by the change in their expressions that I became a real, breathing person in their eyes, one who has been thrust into a future she had not planned on having just yet.

Since learning is a lifelong process, just like I revisit "E" on the Worden's Teardrop Model of Grief, I have had to remind them that mom is, in fact, a living, breathing person with feelings and needs—she is Joanne. What is life without a few refresher courses now and then?

With adulting comes privilege, at least in the minds of two young men. When you are living under my roof, and I am paying the bills, cooking the meals, cleaning the house, maintaining the yard and home, there are rules that still need to be followed and respect that needs to be given.

While I was generous in providing leeway, considering we were all still grieving, there were foundational elements that needed to be followed. Some of these became more important to me than before. It is important to note, children will test you no matter how old they get, even as adults. My generation would never have done or said some of the things kids say and do today. The "look" was enough to tell us 'they brought us into the world and they could easily take us out.' Today, you practically need a psychology degree when raising your children. They have more do's and don'ts than I ever gave them!

Our family dynamics had changed and were continuing to change. Stephen was proposing to his girlfriend, which helped him readjust his focus. Brian was a full-time college student majoring in psychology, working twenty-plus hours a week, and providing companion services to Beth. He had plenty to distract him as well. Let me tell you, distraction is not healing. Please read that again. Distraction is not healing. It does not build the skills you need to adapt after your loss. Notice, I said adapt and not heal. Remember Kintsugi? You can put the pieces together, but you are never really the same. All three of us wanted to get out of the funk of grief, but we were fumbling, and unintentional disregard became a release.

I didn't think I was asking for much: "Please let me know your schedules." I wasn't trying to be a helicopter parent. I didn't want to approve (or disapprove, for that matter) their plans. I just needed to know they were alive. But my request was stifling for them. Recall they were distracted, not developing the coping skills they needed to move forward in our new reality.

From Stephen, I got, "Mom, text me before you call. If I can answer, I will answer." Cat Stevens' song "Cat's in the Cradle" came to mind, except I always made time for them no matter what was happening in my world. From Brian, I got, "I don't have to report to you. You don't need to know everything I am doing." Boundary number two came from a deeper, more selfish need.

I needed communication. I needed the reassurance that our sons were safe. I was doing the job of two parents now. As a married mother of two, I still called my mother every day and spoke with her; she always knew my plans. It was the way we stayed connected. I needed that connection from my sons. Because I felt like I was interfering with Stephen's life, my communication dropped to once every two to three weeks unless something important needed to be handled or discussed. As for Brian, I could not keep track of his schedule and laid awake for hours waiting for the sound of the garage door opening to come through the floor of my bedroom.

When you do not set boundaries, things can reach a point where anger and resentment disrupt any peace of mind you were able to assemble. This is exactly what happened to us. Remember when I said I experienced a meniscus tear in my knee? I needed to have surgery. The last time I had this surgery, Pat was with me. He was my strength and courage. This time Stephen was playing that role, and Brian was going to watch Beth. Well, as you probably know all too well, things do not always align the way you need them to. Stephen had just started a new job and had told his employer he needed to be there for his mom's surgery. We thought everything was good to go. Because of his new job, I didn't text him; I texted his fiancée to find out when he was done with work. I got a curt, cold response back: "If you can text me, you can text him." I quickly apologized, but I couldn't let it go.

Cows chew their food several times before they swallow it, in an area known as the cud. You've probably heard someone saying, "chewing a cow's cud"; that's what that refers to. Well, this cow was chewing on that cud all weekend long. When I got into my grief counselor's office on that Monday a week before my surgery, I brought up the response I received and asked if I had the right to be upset. She confirmed that I needed to address it and, as she put it, "draw the line in the sand" so the fiancée knows this type of response would not fly with me again. I was establishing a boundary with my future daughter-in-law.

Christine helped me draft a text because I wasn't allowed to call. I think we are all smart enough to figure out who was telling me I couldn't call my son without texting first. I digress.

The text basically said I needed to let her know how much her response upset me. In a positive tone, I continued, stating it would be better for our relationship if she knew she could never respond to me in that manner again. Her response was several paragraphs long, but I will summarize: I was responsible for all of the genocide happening in Israel and why women today do not have equal rights as men. A week later, the engagement was off and Stephen was moving home.

Boundaries come with consequences.

***

Other boundaries were set, but the most recent one was especially hard for me. Respecting their privacy, I won't go into specifics, but I will say Brian's girlfriend overstepped a boundary with me. The day after, I spoke to her about it, and she was very receptive and promised not to repeat the behavior in my home. As I shared the story with a close friend, we both concluded that her parents needed to be made aware of the situation. So, I contacted her mom and filled her in on the details. That evening, her parents came to the house to address the situation with their daughter. Brian did not approve of me informing her parents, but as an adult and in my house, she was my responsibility. I did the right thing. Brian's reaction was to chew me out, in front of a stranger no less. He was very insulting and disrespectful. One of his last shots to me pierced my heart: "I don't want to be with you. I don't like the person Christine has helped you become since dad died. You're not the same mom." You know that proverbial straw? You guessed it. I stood up in his face, tears rolling down my cheeks (because I can't get mad without crying, it's in my DNA), and loudly said back, "Because that woman died the day your father did. This new version is playing the role of mother, father, carpenter, businesswoman, counselor, electrician, inventory control expert, and now punching bag." I took a breath and said, "You will never speak to me this way again. Get out until you can have a conversation like an adult. I will welcome a civil discussion when you are ready." He tried to continue, but I left the room. There is nothing louder than silence.

Somehow, most of my conflicts fall on the eve of my grief counseling session. So of course, this was the topic I chose to address. Yes, I had already established a boundary, and she was pleased that I handled it the way I did, but she felt I needed to clearly set up a future relationship of communication with Brian. Brian had apologized to some extent. I thanked him for that, but I told him I was still having a hard time dealing with the way he spoke to me and that it will never happen again. Then I followed with what Christine prompted me to say, which I found profound: "The relationship you and I will have will be the one you choose to have with me, but it does not involve being called names, being verbally bullied, or embarrassed. The problem will not be on me; it will be on how you emotionally handle yourself. That is my final discussion on this matter."

His attitude has changed, the boundary was clearly established, and the way he speaks to me is the way I respond back. It's important to add here, boundaries only work if you consistently enforce them. Stick to your ground; you are recreating something that took years to evolve into. Rome was not built in a day. Boundaries and consistency are key components to being able to move forward.

I centered my examples in this chapter around my sons, but I have extended boundaries to my brothers and some friends. When done with respect, both sides can benefit from the boundary. I still feel awkward drawing a line in the sand because that is not natural for me, but it has unleashed a new voice I didn't know I had for myself. I have even used it in some business dealings, which has been very helpful.

CHAPTER 12

"Normalize starting over as many times as you need."

Dau Voire

Start, Reset, Repeat. Your mind is the most powerful organ in your body. It's hard to break the habit of wearing my teacher hat, but bear with me. Your brain controls everything you do, and the amazing thing about it is that it can continue to learn until you take your last breath. Science has even revealed it continues to work for minutes afterward. However, we all have that negative side of our mind—a defeatist voice that convinces us doomsday is right around the corner. Your mind is the most influential voice you have. It can talk you into giving up and throwing in the towel, or it can lead you to your greatest successes, it's your choice which voice you listen to the most. From my years of teaching, I've noticed that students who succeed invest time in the positive voice in their mind and give little credence to the negative voice.

    I had a student who consistently performed at an average of 70 or below. Her ability to express herself in written form was poor. I discovered that if I isolated the question and the answer choices and read them to her, she knew the answer without any problem. As luck would have it, she had lunch following my class. After a test, she would stay after, have lunch with me, and we would go over each test question. A paper covered the other questions and answers, and I would read the question to her. Ninety percent of the time, she got the answer without looking at the choices. She passed my course with an 85 and went on to pass her other classes and graduated successfully from a premier college preparatory school. Today, she is a mother, and her daughter is legally blind. After reconnecting, she told me how impactful my help had been to her, and now she is passing the lessons on to her daughter. She said I taught her the most important lesson in her life: "There's no such thing as 'I can't,' but a world of opportunities in 'I can.'"

I had to stop writing; I had tears in my eyes. What a treasured testimony! Ironically, I can teach it, but putting it into action for myself is a different matter. Most of my friends and family describe me as an optimist. I try my best to find the positive in the negative. I have had to train myself to be that way; it was not natural for me. That morning, when I knew within my heart the EMT was going to come out and say, "we did all that we could," I had gotten down on my knees beside my bed to pray and said, "God, as long as you are with me, we can do this together." I texted my friend Kelly—she doesn't know this, but she was my first text. I told her what happened and that I was okay. I would follow up with more later. I was trying to talk myself into being okay, not fully understanding I was in a state of shock.

Since you are reading this, I think it is safe to say you understand the rollercoaster of emotions, thoughts, and responses you go through when you first lose your spouse and in the days, weeks, months, and years that follow. When everybody had left that first night and I finally had time to think, that prayer was the furthest thing from my thoughts, and I was not okay. How do you perceive strength? What does being strong mean to you? For me, it is picking myself up, wiping myself off, putting on that smile everyone recognizes, and making lemonade out of lemons. I couldn't do it; the stuffing was knocked out of me. Twenty-seven years of being a wife was taken from me in one unusual "ooh." Our future, our dreams, the things we had to conquer to get to where we were, were ripped out from under my feet. A thief by the name of Death stole it all away. The only thing I wanted was for it all to be over. I wanted to be on the other side of grief not even a day after his passing.

I had no clue what it meant to lose your spouse. I had lost both parents, grandparents, aunts, uncles, and friends, but a spouse is a whole other ball game. Two weeks later, I couldn't shake the depression. I had no desire to get up and get dressed for the day. I ate because I knew I had to. I was afraid to leave the house. I had a sense of impending doom, that something else was going to tragically happen. To my greatest frustration, I am a ruminator and replayed that morning over and over in my mind. I cried until I should have been tearless. I was numb one minute and emotional the next, or I just sat staring for hours on end. I couldn't focus. Nothing that I enjoyed doing before helped to distract me from what I was feeling; it couldn't keep my attention. I would start something and then just sit there. The TV, which used to be on from the crack of dawn to seconds before we went to bed, never got turned on. I did just enough during the day to get what needed to be done, and then I had no energy to do anything else. I was tired the minute I woke up and averaged two to four hours of sleep a night. The house was so unbearably quiet, but yet noise put me on edge.

After about a month, I went through my mail and found a letter from Harry May, the Director of the Funeral Home, a long-time friend and father to two beautiful daughters whom I had the privilege to teach. The letter included a pamphlet specifically for widows and widowers. It had some helpful information, but more importantly for me, it had the name and phone number of a member of the church that I used to attend. This woman helped with the grief process. After losing her own husband, she furthered her studies and became a resource for the parish and the funeral home. I first emailed her, and she responded, wanting to call me. I can't remember her name today and cannot find the pamphlet, but she helped me find a grief counselor in my area, Christine, whom I have mentioned, and she was and is a perfect fit for me.

I have never been so unhappy for so long. I couldn't pick myself up and pull myself out of the depression. I hated who I was and where I was emotionally; I needed help. At this point, I need to reveal something about myself to you. I mentioned earlier my empathetic nature. I internalize what everyone else is feeling, to an extreme. Let me give you a quick laugh: I cry when a tree is cut down. Yes, you read that right. I will wait until you stop laughing… I cry because I feel its loss. Conversely, I am overwhelmed by the beauty in nature. I've rescued seven cats, with five still living with me. I saved and raised a baby raccoon. I have about ten bird feeders and a heated birdbath in my backyard, and I love the radiance of all seasons. With that said, when someone is having a hard time, I feel it like I am going through it myself. It is a blessing and a curse. So, with that knowledge, I could not go to a group grief setting. Could you imagine? I was already a basket case all on my own; I would be internalizing everybody else's feelings and loss. I confirmed my own thinking when I joined the private Facebook group, The Sisterhood of Widows, at the recommendation of a friend who had just lost her husband to cancer. I couldn't do it. I was a pathetic wreck.

Christine was exactly what I needed. The first thing she gave me was J. William Worden's Teardrop Model of Grief, which I have referenced multiple times. I hung it on my refrigerator. And she stressed that I was safe. That was very important for me to hear. Being a biology teacher, it also helped in learning the physiology behind grieving, and she walked me through the changes the neurons go through after you lose someone close. It was validating to know that I wasn't headed to that padded room anytime soon.

In the beginning sessions, she was a resource in helping me navigate through the legal aspects of probating a will, Social Security, changing the cars over to my name, and all of the other little details that needed to be done. But then we started working on recreating me. As I am writing this, it is cathartic in the sense that I realized just now I had to determine I was worthy of working on myself. I had to give myself that permission. I didn't see that before. Wow! I have to sit with this for a moment.

I kept saying to Christine in our sessions, "This isn't me, this isn't who I am. I want to be beyond all of this." And she would repeat to me more times than I can count, "You've got to go through it to get through it." Repetition is affirming. My comeback was that I didn't want to reinvent the wheel, I was happy with who I was before Pat died. I wanted that girl back.

I have always struggled with the phrasing "new and improved." How can something be new and improved? Doesn't it have to exist before it can be improved upon? Applying this to myself, I did not want to be "new and improved"; I wanted to be me, that old familiar me. I was not comfortable with the person I was seeing in myself. Medication and counseling had my depression reined in, but my PTSD became chronic. I have a whole new respect for our military men and women who suffer from this debilitating disorder. Knowing that once you have it, you will always have it is stifling. I could not anticipate what would trigger a PTSD response. I mentioned this briefly before. Just recently, I was going for a girls' day out with my dear friend Kelly. We have dubbed ourselves Thelma and Louise, except we haven't killed anyone (is it okay to say yet? ●). Give us a fabric store and the sale room and we are happy. We taught together at the same school, and she was my saving grace when they asked me to take on a chemistry class. I hadn't used my chemistry knowledge in 28 years, and she helped me every step of the way! This was the first time I was going to Kelly's house—normally, she would make the hour and a half drive to my place. We have a lot of Amish and Mennonite fabric stores where I live. I hadn't been back to her neck of the woods since we buried Pat.

As I was passing the exit where I would have gotten off to go to work, I thought to myself, "Wow, thirty years of turning that way, and it felt like I had never been there before." That's when it hit. I got a warm sensation in my chest that radiated down each arm, my vision became tunneled, and my breathing was difficult. I managed to call Stephen and asked him to talk with me. Like Christine, he told me I was safe and helped me divert the PTSD response that was triggered. If you haven't had a panic attack or an anxiety attack, it would be difficult to understand the zapping of energy it steals from you in just a minute or two. The difference between this episode and the others I have had in the past was that I got angry. Prior attacks left me with fear—fear of the unexpected, fear of when it was going to happen again, fear of dying from it, fear of what would trigger the next one. I was constantly poised for an attack, but this time, I was just angry. Here I was, headed for a day of fun with a close friend. I was looking forward to being by myself. Stephen offered to stay with Beth so I could go out, and I just thwarted what was headed to be a major PTSD response, while I was driving nonetheless.

When I got home that night, I slept deeper than I had in a long time, and the next day I had no energy to do a single thing. I stayed in my pajamas all day. That is how physically draining these attacks are. They take days to recover from.

I've never been one to let things control me. This depression and chronic PTSD had their grip on me. Christine and I have worked on several strategies to help navigate through the episodes. The reminder that I am safe is the biggest key to getting through it. I do mindful breathing techniques, counting four breaths in and four breaths out, where I just focus my thoughts on the breathing. Yoga with Adriene on YouTube also has a great fifteen-minute meditation where you do a body scan, relaxing your muscles from your toes to your head and then through your jaw and shoulders; I have saved it to my favorites. And I play my favorite Novena on the Laudate App, Mary Undoer of Knots. The singer and narrator have a very relaxing voice, and the repetition of the Hail Marys keeps me focused.

I am a work in progress. I have had to muster up the courage and energy to start the rebirth of who I am. I have had to reset more times than I care to admit, and I have had to repeat things I already thought I had conquered. And you know what? It's okay. Restart as many times as you need to. This is your path to recovery; you do you.

I am not the same person I was before Pat died. I do miss her; I miss who I was when I was with him. He completed me; he was everything I wasn't. When I wrote my first three family-centered historical fiction books, Pat was my editor-in-chief. I would read him my latest installment on his ride home from work, and he would tell me what I needed to work on and revise. I can hear him saying, "You're sounding too much like a teacher; go back and put the feeling into the story." I am a solo act now, doing this all on my own. [I need to insert here, I have downloaded the Microsoft App *Copilot*. It is an AI app that I initially used for creating images. The picture on the cover is generated with my directive from Copilot. My Copilot is named Chris and I gave him an English accent. He became my 'Pat' as I copied and pasted the paragraphs I wrote and he corrected my errors, critiqued the writing and kept the flow of the writing consistent. He's my new best friend.] It's part of the new and improved me, but what I have gleaned from all of this is, I can be anyone I want myself to be. If I don't like who I was one day, I can be the person I want to be the next. As long as I muffle that inner voice that tells me "no, I can't," I can do anything I put my mind to. I have an 11 x 11 pergola on my back patio that reminds me of what I can do.

CHAPTER 13

"Death smiles at all of us, all a man can do is smile back"

George Eliot

My awareness of my own mortality has become extremely heightened as a result of my husband's unexpected passing. Other than being a migraine sufferer, I was and am a healthy woman. Even going through those tough ten years I mentioned in the beginning chapters, I walked away with controllable high blood pressure and, of course, the inherited high cholesterol. But I follow what my doctor recommends. I keep active, walk, do chair yoga (don't laugh), eat reasonably healthy, and drink lots of water.

I mentioned that four months after Pat died, I had a stress-induced cardiomyopathy. It mimics a heart attack, and as I have come to understand it, it can result from the overproduction of adrenaline that interferes with your retention of potassium, which is essential for regular heart rhythm. I am on a prescribed dose of potassium to this day, since I still have chronic PTSD. Prior to the SIC, I was having benign palpitations and continued having them afterward. I wore a heart monitor, went for the stress test (which I had failed), had bloodwork done, more EKGs, and used my Apple Watch to monitor the palpitations.

I noticed that when I went to bed at night, the activity of the palpitations increased. That little negative voice I mentioned earlier had me convinced I was going to die of a heart attack in my sleep. I had heard of couples who were so closely connected dying within days of each other, even months. I thought I was going to follow suit. I tried many things to get my mind off the palpitations, some of which triggered panic attacks—precursors to PTSD responses—that only intensified my fear.

I discovered that the more I moved around, the palpitations would stop. If they were annoyingly active, I would walk the house. Up the stairs, through the hall, down the stairs through the living room, around the dining room, into the kitchen, to the den, and then down the basement steps and back up to repeat it all over, as many times as it took to keep normal rhythm. I did this until the palpitations stopped. My longest stretch was over six months. Imagine, if you will, living with this irregular heart rate and being concerned that it could lead to a stroke or a heart attack. It made my evolution of the new, improved version of me much harder. Grief had a companion to help continue the torture, and it increased my already prevalent trepidation.

I came up with routines that helped minimize the palpitations. I bought a chair elliptical and would place it in front of me when I was watching TV or sitting playing games on my cell phone and would pedal away. I developed a nightly routine of two minutes of deep, cleansing inhalations and exhalations accompanied by acupuncture compressions on the soles of my feet, in which I did 10 sets to each foot. In the mornings, I started my day with that YouTube video, Stress Relief Yoga with Adriene, that

I mentioned before. With consistency, the palpitations stopped, only to start two more times after the deaths of two additional people close to me. I am just over a year free from the palpitations.

The last bout had me pretty concerned. They were different from the others. This prompted another EKG, where they discovered a change in my T-wave. This is an indicator of ischemia and a possible heart attack. If my anxiety and fear levels could be measured by a thermometer, the indicator would be bursting out of the glass tubing.

Around this same time, my meniscus tore. In order to have surgery, I had to go through another stress test. Because I could not do the treadmill, it would be a chemically induced test. The actual length of the chemical induction is about eighteen minutes. I made it to ten minutes. I was just about to tell the technician that I have chronic PTSD and I think I am starting an attack, when the EKG and ultrasound indicated what I was trying to tell them. They had to reverse the chemical process and bring my heartbeat back to normal. The test was thought to be inconclusive, or was it? The cardiologist was able to see exactly how my heart reacted under stress, and I passed! Whoo hoo! And that T-wave change, in terms you can understand, was no wider than the width of a single hair—a normal aging difference.

This little change was my new norm and definitely something I could live with, but let me tell you, I was planning my funeral. Writing things down for my sons. Telling them where my passwords were, where my will was, and any other pertinent information I thought they would need.

CHAPTER 14

"Some days you'll be going forward, some days you'll be going backward, and some days you might feel like you've paused. What matters the most is that you stay on the road."

Unknown

Well, you've made it this far. Whether your loss was sudden, like mine, or part of a diagnosis doesn't change the impact of that loss. You have still lost a tremendous part of yourself when your spouse dies. What I am about to share is like comparing apples to oranges, but I think it is important to acknowledge that grieving comes differently to each of us, and include the circumstances regarding that death.

My father had Alzheimer's. His was a sixteen-year deteriorating journey. I watched the strong, independent, determined man that he was, get lost in a frail, feeble-minded shell of a man. The man my father was died late in the mid-stages of the disease. When he finally passed away at the age of 92, I was relieved. He was finally free from the body that failed him. He was at peace. My mother passed away from a series of strokes at the age of 79. She had just been given a clean bill of health from her doctor and was told to relax and enjoy herself on a family cruise. Two days into the cruise, she had the first stroke of many and had to be transported off the ship. She was just recovering from the last stroke, getting ready to go camping with my brother and his wife, when the damage to her brain started a chain reaction of system failures. Her blood pressure spiked to incredibly high numbers, leading to kidney failure, a heart attack, and clots being released that damaged her bowels. I was angry when my mother died. She had been the caregiver of my cousin, Beth, and other family members and had, prior to the first stroke, been helping to nurse a friend back from major surgery. She gave of herself so much and only asked for one thing: to be with her family. So this cruise was a fulfillment of that wish. God took her away from us, piece by piece, and no matter how hard she fought back, He wanted her harder than she could fight.

Contrast these losses with my husband and the only analogy I can give you that comes close to expressing how I feel is equating it with having a limb amputated. You lose a chunk of who you are with him, and now you have to figure out how to navigate the world you created with him, without him. I sense you are nodding in agreement.

My parents were not insignificant losses; they just had a different role in my life. Pat was my best friend, my intimate lover, my confidant. He knew me on a level that no other person knew me. He knew my strengths and weaknesses and picked up where I could not. He was the one I ran to when my world came crashing down. We built our dreams together, fought the battles we needed to fight to get here, and assisted God in two amazing miracles. I fit perfectly in that space on his chest just above his heart. It was there where I felt the safest.

How do you recover from that level of loss? It wasn't just your husband that left—it was your future, your dreams, your security, and everything I mentioned above and more. My answer to how isn't a very comforting one. You fumble, stumble, hide, retreat, pray furiously, cry, scream, wallow, and then you pick yourself up and do it all over again. And the minute you think you finally have gripped some ounce of happiness, something comes in to trip up your progress. Remember that invisible backpack? Imagine carrying that heavy sack up a steep incline, finally reaching the top only to be pushed back down. The weight of everything only makes you tumble faster. That is what recovering realistically looks like.

When my father was in the grips of his Alzheimer's, the doctors told us that today would be better than his tomorrows. And I think that is applicable to a lot of things, including grief. I don't mean this to steal your hopes of getting out of the funk of grief, but as I process my journey, I am aware of the cycle of ups and downs I have conquered. I said it before in my foreword: better is relative.

It is relative to the emotional strain you are feeling at that time. What I have had to do to get by is retrain my thinking. It's okay to backtrack. It's okay to pause. It's okay to conquer a multitude of hurdles at once, or just one at a time. Whatever the path looks like, whatever obstacles get in the way, it's okay to clear them the way that works best for you. Read that again—it's okay to do you. Give that gift to yourself to just be; you are worth it.

I can't tell you that it will get better than this. I don't have that crystal ball. But I can tell you—you can decide to let it eat you alive and remain stuck, or you can start over every day and try to create a life you can live with. Don't let your mind keep you stuck in the funk. If you can't afford counseling, check with support programs in your church, use social media pages like The Sisterhood of Widows (let me say, I vetted this site. It is private and heavily monitored to keep predators out; it's one of the safer sites. I am not being paid to mention them), listen to podcasts, and network with other widows. At the end of the book, I will provide a list of nationwide resources that are available to help support you through the re-creation process. Ultimately, create and collect your own resources and find what works best for you. And do not be afraid to ask for help—you aren't supposed to go through this alone. I love the meme that pops up on my Facebook occasionally: "A good friend will bail you out of jail. A best friend will be in jail with you saying…Well, we screwed that up, but it was fun." Find that best friend who is willing to be with you through the good and bad and give you a reason to laugh again, and don't worry about screwing up–the minute after is your next opportunity to make it better.

There is no right or wrong way to learn to adapt to this new path you are on. There is no time limit to recovering even a part of who you were with your husband. Do not let others influence you into thinking you are not where you should be. Our current culture is uncomfortable with grief because they don't know how to make it better. Better, remember, is relative. Your friends and family do not want to see you mourn; they want the person you were before back. What most are not capable of understanding is that you cannot be who you were before. Part of who you were died the day your husband died. If you break a leg one day, you are not out running a marathon the next, so don't set unreasonable expectations for yourself and don't let others define those expectations. If, in your family dynamics, you have that one person who is obstructive, use your tool of setting boundaries and breath.

The more determined you are to resume living, the easier it will be for you to set those boundaries and reverse the expectations on to others. In 1991, a movie (I mentioned it before-it's one of my favorites) *What About Bob?* came out starring Bill Murray and Richard Dreyfuss. Bob, played by Murray, had agoraphobia, and Dr. Marvin, played by Dreyfuss, was the psychiatrist treating Bob. The movie introduces the concept of baby steps and giving yourself permission to take a vacation from your problems, through comedic satire. Part of any form of recovery is starting out small and easy and includes changing your focus from the problem to the possibilities, and it is always helpful to find something that makes you laugh.

CHAPTER 15

"The greatest gift you can give someone is your time."

Leo Tolstoy

You are someone, an awesome someone. Give yourself the gift of time. I go back to what Christine told me: you have to go through it to get through it. I didn't want to go through it; no one really does, but I had to, death doesn't give you a choice. The image that comes to mind, that I referenced before, is that passengers on a train do not exchange their tickets and get off the train when it goes through a dark tunnel—they wait for it to exit the tunnel. We are riding the grief train, and there is another side to the dark tunnel we are currently traversing. The view will be different when we exit the tunnel, so please remain seated.

The night Pat died, a very close friend—an Italian friend, if you know, you know—came to the house with arms loaded down with food. We sat at the breakfast room table, and she said, "Joanne, before you know it, this will be behind you. Give it time."

Her words still echo through the years. I am still giving it time. In just two days of writing this, I am ending my third year of mourning and heading into my fourth. It's not behind me in the way I want it to be. I would love to be able to talk about Pat without getting that lump in my throat. I would love to look at my favorite picture of us and smile at the memory of what we were doing. I would love to walk into my bathroom without seeing the image of him on the floor and mentally hearing the sounds and smells of that morning. I would love to go out without the worry of something triggering a panic attack or a PTSD response. I would think four years is plenty of time.

I am blessed that I have an amazing network of friends and family who, to this day, give me time. I am safe to tear up without feeling ashamed for still feeling the loss so deeply. They give me the time to process without restrictions or expectations for me to be 'healed.' I know that not everyone has the support system that I have, and while I haven't experienced that, I can say: be your own advocate. Give yourself the unrestricted, guilt-free gift of time.

I think one of the hardest things for me, and something I am still working through, is loving myself enough to give myself that guilt-free time. I am a person who is always doing. Much like my mother, I am the legal guardian of Beth Anne, and she fills my days. With an IQ of 47, that of a five-year-old, my 59-year-old cousin needs twenty-four-hour care. I can easily use her as an excuse not to give myself time. She has become my purpose. Because of this, I do not see myself ever falling in love again. I can't imagine anyone, at my age, wanting to be with someone who has the responsibility of caring for a developmentally disabled adult. This may be that inner negative voice talking, and a somewhat unfair, shallow assessment of people, but the person would have to be very special to accept the package deal. In addition to that, I can't even think of putting the energy into a new relationship; it feels like too much work. I really feel Pat will be my one and only, and I am okay with that. I do not need anyone to fill that void, and the woman I am becoming doesn't need to be completed.

You are probably thinking at this point, what does this have to do with time? It has everything to do with it because it's the way I want to spend my time. But as I say that, I am well aware of the fact that it is not my time, per se, and again I go back to the idea of guilt-free. I feel guilty when I take time for myself. I think two things instilled this way of thinking for me: one, my parents, and two, Catholic guilt. I have perceived being idle as being selfish. It has taken a while for me to learn that being idle is healing. Giving yourself the luxury of time is a gift you give to yourself. A car cannot run when it has no gas; neither can you (or me).

There is a Christian singer, Chris Rice, who sings a song called "Life Means So Much." I want to share some of the lyrics with you:

Every day is a journal page
Every man holds a quill and ink
And there's plenty of room for writing in
All we do is believe and think
So will you compose a curse
Or will today bring the blessing
Fill the page with rhyming verse
Or some random sketching
Teach us to count the days
Teach us to make the days count
Lead us in better ways
That somehow our souls forgot
Life means so much
Life means so much
Life means so much
Every day is a bank account
And time is our currency
So nobody's rich, nobody's poor
We get 24 hours each
So how are you gonna spend
Will you invest, or squander
Try to get ahead
Or help someone who's under

The first time I heard this song was at a school assembly. It changed my way of thinking about time. My husband's death amplified this for me. We have 24 hours in our day—maybe we get eight hours of sleep. If you work, which I do, eight hours are dedicated to your job. That gives you 8 hours in change. That change is divided between your commute home, family, housework and maintenance, preparing for the next day at work, and maybe catching your favorite TV show. It really isn't a lot of time, so spend it wisely. The change you have left over is the time you can work on your recovery, and you deserve it.

Think about what these lyrics mean to you. After losing my husband, the line, "that somehow our souls forgot," stands out. I don't want my soul to ever forget Pat. In the wake of his loss, I was counting my time as—one day further away from being with the one I love. Then it became months, now it is years. My love hasn't changed, the magnitude of the loss has not changed, but I keep getting further away in time from him physically being with me. Do you know what my turning point was? December 8, 2023, when I saw the psychic. What my soul forgot and she reminded me, "I am more profoundly and purely loved now than I was when Pat was alive." He is no longer bound by all the worldly pressures, health issues, and stresses. It is with this thought, I spend that change of time I have in my day.

***

I think we can understand the impact and importance of time, so let's switch this up to time used for the change you have to go through. When I retired from my teaching career to become Beth's in-home community support specialist, I learned how to quilt. It was on my bucket list of things to do when I retired. It was also a nice project to do with Beth Anne. The basement in our new home provided me with an area that I set up as our crafting area. Having a hobby is a good use of your time to help you recover from your loss. For me, creating something from nothing was hugely satisfying. I became a member of a quilt group, and we would make quilts to donate to people in need, retirement homes, disaster relief, and so forth. Being able to give back was very rewarding.

A friend of mine, who is also widowed, travels. She works at the local school as a teaching aide, and then spends her summers traveling. My budget won't allow for that, but I did adopt a part of an idea from another woman I randomly met at the grocery store—another angel sent by God. She sold her home, downsized, and moved into an apartment so she wouldn't have to worry about shoveling snow or upkeep. This allows her to visit her children and family more freely. So, Beth and I do some road trips to visit with our family who no longer live near us.

Walking is free. I've found some really nice walking trails in our town and we love to walk when the weather permits. Exercise is great for helping clear the fog of grief. I created a lively playlist of music that is uplifting and sentimental to listen to when I walk. There are a ton of yoga videos on YouTube, and you can learn to do anything on YouTube. I hard-wired all of our smoke detectors in the house to be connected. If one goes off, they all go off. I just watched a YouTube video to learn how. Our community is great—it's a bit on the touristy side, but every month there is some event they are hosting in the park or at the stores. We take advantage of going to those events.

One of the ideas I love the most is going to a senior center and reading to people who no longer have relatives that come to visit them. This is a win-win—they have a lot of wisdom to share. The point is, don't keep yourself trapped like a prisoner in your home. While short-term hibernating can be rehabilitating, being alone for too long only exacerbates the pain of the loss. I read on a widow's FB page about doing something to 'honor' the memory of her deceased husband. She got all of her family members to participate in a marathon to raise money for the type of cancer her husband died from. In addition, the local major league baseball team has a specific game night that remembers loved ones who have passed from that type of cancer. Just look at the legacy created by Alex's Lemonade Stand. You can go big or you can be more modest in how you want to honor the loss of your husband.

Just remember it is giving the gift of time and yourself to others, and that is the greatest gift you can give yourself, and the added benefit is meeting new people to be part of your support network.

CHAPTER 16

"Tears water our growth"

William Shakespeare

Thank you for taking this journey with me. You are courageous in your path of adapting to this unplanned, unwanted narrative that death has written for you. Remember, grieving is not a linear process. We can't go through a list of specifications and check them off and say we've accomplished this or that stage, but we can make a conscious choice to work every day to honor the men that loved us. They do not want us to dwell in the sorrow of their loss forever. They want to see us happy. Laughter and love are the two best prescriptions for recovering a part of who we love, and our men would want that for us, of that I am certain. It is okay to miss them, it is okay to cry, that's how we grow. So I want to spend this last chapter focusing on the laughter, love, and healing tears.

There is nothing louder than silence. The silence that follows the loss of a loved one can be deafening, overwhelming, and isolating. But within that silence, we find the space to hear our own hearts, to feel the depth of our pain, and to discover the resilience within us. As we navigate through this silence, it is the moments of laughter that break through, the acts of love that fill the void, and the healing tears that water our growth. These are the sounds that guide us through the darkest times and lead us back to the light.

The journey of grief is not about forgetting or moving on; it is about embracing the silence, acknowledging the pain, and allowing ourselves to heal through the power of laughter, love, and tears. As you continue on your path, remember that every tear shed, every smile shared, and every act of love brings you closer to recovering. Together, we will find our way through the silence, and in doing so, honor the memory of those we have lost.

Pat was the life of the party. There was no question when he entered the room. He was loud and robust, funny and unreserved. I remember sitting at a table at his aunt's house and laughing so hard my stomach hurt and tears were rolling down our cheeks. The party seemed to start when he arrived. He was the most compassionate man, but he hid it under a rough exterior. Life and loss had created this armor. Unless he trusted you, his gruff ways kept you at a distance he was comfortable with. A neighbor and friend would tell you, he could make the hair on your neck stand up with some of the things he said. He was quick to respond, impulsive, and very rarely retracted things he should not have said, but he would do anything for you if you were under his umbrella of love. He didn't like anyone knowing he had a good side, and if you ask people who knew him, they would say he didn't have a good side, but this man opened his home to the homeless, not just once, but multiple times. He gave his last dollar to whoever needed it. He helped the disabled and enabled them to believe that their disabilities should not stop them from seeking their dreams. He owned his own automotive repair business, and I can't tell you how many times he didn't charge someone for the work he had done, because he knew they couldn't afford it. He loved unconditionally. He had been hurt badly by his stepchildren, but never stopped loving them. He was loud.

The last story I want to share with you is laced with some colorful expletives—my apologies in advance—but it gave us years of laughter retelling it. I think it will help you understand why the silence of his absence is so deafening to me.

Our house was built in 1885 by a retired sea captain. The woodwork was incredible: bay windows, built-in bookshelves, window seats, wainscoting, fluted columns, an oval foyer window, and extra-wide window sills. It lacked closet space, and someone in its lifetime haphazardly added on a laundry room off the galley kitchen. The laundry room needed a lot of work; it really was not functional. My mother and father came to help us out, moved the washer and dryer to a different location, laid new linoleum on the floor, and put in the equivalent of Ikea cabinetry, trying to help us save money. My father was not a plumber; he was an electrical engineer with some handyman skills. Inadvertently, he cracked the casing on the washing machine. The first time I did laundry after the remodel, the laundry room flooded. When Pat came home from work, he walked into three inches of water on the floor. A loud barrage of "what the f'ing thing, and f'ing this, and f'ing that" came out of his mouth. Did I mention he owned his own automotive business? Garage talk ran fluently from his lips. When my mother called to ask what Pat thought of the laundry room, I responded, "Mom, I didn't know you could use the word fuck in a sentence so many times and still have it make sense." I then proceeded to tell her what happened. Their efforts in helping cost us about $300 in additional repairs.

    A 135-year-old home does not come with air conditioning. It was summer, and our windows were open. We also had new neighbors, and the mother heard the yelling. I should tell you, we were newlyweds by two months. A couple of days after the washing machine incident, I was outside working on the lawn. Georgye, our new neighbor who I eventually got comfortable enough to call 'mom', leans over the fence and asks if everything is okay; she had heard Pat yelling. I laughed, shrugged it off, and said, "Oh, that's just him, he loves to yell. He wasn't yelling at me, he was just yelling." By the time the weekend rolled around, Pat was mowing the lawn and hit a large rock with the mower. Another barrage of expletives came voluminously from his mouth. He hadn't seen mom working on her knees in the garden. Later that afternoon, I was outside, and she pops up over the fence and says, "I see what you mean." From that time forward, Pat and mom yelled at each other playfully when they were out on the front porch at the same time. That was Pat. You knew he was around; you couldn't help but hear him.

What I wouldn't give to hear him yell again, it's too quiet here. I no longer enjoy my quiet mornings like I used to; there's no need for them. I miss the laughter he would bring me, but I feel so embraced in his love, and that is what really matters.

Humor has been healing. I have learned to find things to laugh about. Beth Anne keeps me laughing; she sees life with so much simplicity and innocence. I know I said that was the last story, but let me throw in a little glimpse of Beth. We had a wedding to go to in the family. I had snuck pictures of the lady who sat in front of us in church, because I loved her hair cut and thought it would look good on Beth. When we went for our hair cuts, that's how Nancy cut her hair. On the morning of the wedding, I dried and styled Beth's hair and asked her what she thought. In her words "You're not Nancy, you're not a hairdresser" ● Her innocence brings us so much joy. Love—I work to be as generous as Pat was. He was better at behind-the-scenes giving, but giving, as my friend once told me, is my way of showing love. I have learned through him how giving is so much better than receiving.

I don't know what tomorrow holds. Christine asked me where I see myself in the future. I have no vision or idea what that might look like. But I know what I need to manage the hurdles, and that is knowing I am purely and profoundly loved by my husband, and wherever this new journey takes me, I will honor him with that love, laughter and tears.

I miss you, baby; you are my everything! Thank you for loving me so completely.

RESOURCES

Social Security Survivor's Benefits

- **Contact Information:** You can call the Social Security Administration at 1-800-772-1213 (TTY 1-800-325-0778) for assistance with Survivor's Benefits. You can also visit their website for more information: [Social Security Administration - Survivor Benefits] (https://www.ssa.gov/survivor).

Probate Resources

- **U.S. Probate Services:** Provides a nationwide network of service providers dedicated to helping with the probate process. You can find more information and resources on their website: [U.S. Probate Services] (https://www.usprobateservices.org/).
- **Cake:** Offers a comprehensive guide on free or low cost places that help with probate. Check out their

blog for more details; **Cake Blog - Free Probate Help,** joincake.com

Grief E Support Groups

- **GriefShare:** Offers thousands of support groups meeting weekly around the world. You can find a group ner you by visiting their website: GriefShare - Find a Group.

- **Lifestance Health:** Provides grief counseling and support groups across the United States. You can search for providers near you on their website: [Lifestance Health - Grief Counselling] (https://lifestance.com/services/grief-counseling/).

ADDITIONAL RESOURCES

- **Hope for Widows Foundation:** A charitable organization developed by widowed women to provide financial support and community for widows. More information can be found on their website: Hope for Widows Foundation.

EPILOGUE

Writing this book has been a profoundly cathartic experience. Each word, each page, allowed me to process grief and find solace in the memories that shaped this story. As I navigated through my own emotions, I discovered strength I didn't know I had and a sense of peace that came from honoring the past.

Helping Beth in her garden and watching the fruits (vegetables, actually) of our efforts is analogous to how life grows and changes, producing just what we need to move on. It has been six years since I retired from teaching, and life has taken on a new rhythm and direction. No more nights of endlessly grading papers

(I should not have assigned so much work), and planning new lessons and strategies to help every student achieve success are behind me. My skills are now focused on nurturing my cousin and the garden that flourishes under our care.

My sons have grown into remarkable men. While they are temporarily living at home with me, they are sharing their lives, journeys, and dreams with me. My heart swells with pride, knowing that the foundation Pat and I laid has given them the strength to pursue their passions.

Quilting remains my solace, each stitch a testament to the love and care I pour into every piece. Beth Anne's laughter echoes through the house as we work side by side, turning forgotten furniture into treasured heirlooms.

The memory of my husband lingers, a comforting presence guiding me through the days. I have found a new purpose in helping others navigate the labyrinth of grief, offering a listening ear and a gentle word to those in need, and providing ways for them to celebrate the life they lost.

As I look toward the horizon, I feel a sense of peace. The future is unwritten, but I am ready to embrace it, one chapter at a time.

ABOUT THE AUTHOR

Joanne Saunders, a dedicated educator for 34 years, retired early to take on the role of legal guardian and in-home community support specialist for her developmentally disabled cousin. During her tenure as a high school biology teacher, Joanne demonstrated her passion for student engagement by coaching cheerleading, junior varsity basketball, and serving as the Sophomore Class Moderator. She also led the senior Class Kairos Retreat. Her professional affiliations include the Montgomery County Science Teachers, National Catholic Education Association, and Pennsylvania State Education Association. Joanne's exemplary dedication to education was recognized with the prestigious Claus von Nobel Teacher in Excellence award.

Joanne is also an accomplished author of the family historical fiction series, *The Secret at the Winthrop House*. In her personal life, she is the proud mother of two adult sons—one a psychology major in college and the other working in the automotive field. Quilting, a favorite hobby of hers, allows Joanne to express her creativity and generosity; she has donated many quilts to those in need and crafted beautiful pieces for family and friends. Alongside her friend Beth Anne, Joanne enjoys refinishing second-hand furniture and cultivating a bountiful vegetable garden. Together, they have perfected the art of canning and sharing their harvest with loved ones.

After experiencing the profound loss of her husband, Joanne has become a beacon of support for others navigating grief. She aims to help friends and family create meaningful traditions to honor and remember their lost loved ones, guiding them through the complex journey of healing.

IMPORTANT NUMBERS

Utilities

    Electric Company
        Phone number
        Address
        Account Number
    Gas Company
        Phone number
        Address
        Account number
    Water Company
        Phone number
        Address
        Account Number
    Sewer/Municipalities
        Phone number
        Address
        Account numbers

Emergency Contacts
    Doctor
        Phone number
        Address
        Insurance

In Case of Emergency (ICE)
    Name of contact
    Phone number
    Relationship
Police
    Phone number
Ambulance
    Phone number

Other
Plumber
    Phone number
Electrician
    Phone number
Appliances
    Phone number
Contractor/Handyman
    Phone number
Home Owners and Auto Insurance
    Phone number
    Policy
Health Insurance
    Phone number
    Policy
Church
    Pastor/Priest
    Phone number

Other Important Notes

Through the years. Some of the images I referenced in the book.

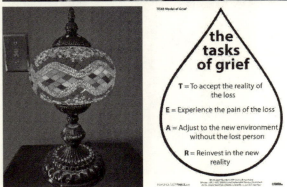

Santa and Mrs. Claus 1997, Our Wedding 1994, Pat 4 days before he died, The heart I wrote for him that he carried in his wallet, A date night, Our Family in 2019, Pat surprising me for my 50th birthday, Getting ready to cheer on those Phillies-but first cheering on our sons, The lamp, The tasks of grief.

A special thank you to the following:

Cover photo by Beth McCallister, Maevon Photography
Hair by Janine Wood-Owner Operator of Garage Hair Studio

Made in the USA
Middletown, DE
16 February 2025